The Literary
Revolution
and Modern Society
and Other Essays

The Literary Revolution and Modern Society and Other Essays

Wilhelm Emrich

Translated by
Alexander and Elizabeth Henderson

FREDERICK UNGAR PUBLISHING CO. • NEW YORK

Translated from the original German as follows:
"Die Literaturrevolution und die moderne Gesellschaft," "Literaturrevolution 1910-1925," and "Schiller und die Antinomien der mensch-
lichen Gesellschaft" (essays 1, 2, and 5) from the volume *Protest
und Verheissung* by Wilhelm Emrich.
"Franz Kafka: Portät," "Franz Kafka zwischen Ost und West," and
"Das Rätsel der Faust II Dichtung" (essays 3, 4, and 6) from the volume *Geist und Widergeist* by Wilhelm Emrich.

By arrangement with the original publishers,
Athenäum Verlag, Frankfurt am Main

Contents

Preface

Contemporary literature and art—i.e. pop art, abstract painting, atonal music, concrete poetry, absolute verse, and the multidimensional novel among others—are the result of an artistic revolution that began as early as 1910, and is thus, by now, sixty years old. Can a sixty-year-old revolution still be called a revolution? Is not such a permanent revolution rather the appropriate expression of the modern industrial society which it professes to fight against?

The following essays attempt to give a critical answer to these questions by revealing the connections between the artistic revolution and industrial society. The first essay describes and analyzes the inner development of the artistic revolution of 1910. By presenting surprisingly similar texts by Rilke and Kafka, it demonstrates

the coming together of subject and object. Man becomes an object, the object in turn becomes an all-
powerful subject dominating man, so that a permanent,
irremediable dialectic evolves between the individual
and society out of which the "absurd" shapes of modern
literature and art, as well as the contradictions between
"concrete" and "abstract" art, or between object worship
and unsubstantiality, may be explained.

The second essay probes the historical genesis of the
artistic revolution of 1910, with its faithful continuation
of the tendencies and artistic principles which had already been developed in naturalism and impressionism.
At the same time—within the framework of a critical
analysis of Georg Lukács's socialist realism and critique
of expressionism—an attempt is made to determine posi-
tively the revolutionary content of this artistic upheaval
with its seemingly highly contradictory programs (including the "program of programlessness" in Dadaism).

The next two essays about Franz Kafka point to the
possibilities of overcoming the hopeless dialectic between the individual and society shown in the first ar-
ticle, and the possible attainment of a change in consciousness that grants the human being sovereignty
over himself and his object world.

This sovereignty—as a possible and realizable demand even in classical literature—is already elucidated
in the essay "Schiller and the Antinomies of Human Society." To Schiller, modern society consists of "barbarians" and "savages." The barbarians strive to create a

totally sensible, harmonious, and free society by the revolutionary destruction of the existing one. The savages conform to and accept, without criticism, the ruthless competition of the establishment. Both stages may be overcome by a new, supreme consciousness in which reason and sensuousness, revolution and conformism, are suspended and transformed into the third stage, which allows a positive evolutionary change of society by permanently reconciling the demands of reason and the sensual needs of man. Only in this third stage does man become human, a free being, freely shaping himself and his society. This third stage is already discernible today in that human art which—in a free play of the imagination—bridges the gap between reason and sensuality.

The true meaning of all this for the history of mankind and the problems of its society becomes evident in the last essay, dealing with the second part of Goethe's *Faust*. This essay illustrates the role played by the arts in shaping history and human society by showing Goethe's symbolic portrayal of the course of three thousand years of European history, from archaic early antiquity to the age of modern technology. Art emerges not only as antithesis and as protest against the catastrophes and horrors of human history and society, but also as a guiding symbol for society's positive formation.

W. E.

November, 1970
Translated by Ursula Lamm

1

The Literary
Revolution
and Modern Society

Between 1904 and 1910, Rilke wrote *The Notebook of
Malte Laurids Brigge,* in which the following sentences
occur:

He knew that he was now departing from everything, not only
from people. In another moment, everything will have lost its
meaning, and this table and the cup and the chair he clutched,
all the neighborly things of everyday will have become incomprehensible and alien and difficult. . . . If my fear were not so
great, I would take comfort in the thought that it is not impossible to see everything differently and yet to live. But I am afraid,
I am unspeakably afraid of this change. After all, I have not even
settled down yet in this world which seems to me a good one.
What would I do in another? I should so much like to remain
among the meanings I have come to cherish, and if change there
must be, I should at least like to be allowed to live among the
dogs, which have a world akin to ours and the same things. For
a while yet I can write all this down and say it. But a day will
come when my hand will be far from me, and when I bid it

write, will write words I do not mean. The time of the different interpretation will dawn, and there shall not be left one word upon the other, and all meaning will dissolve like clouds and descend like water.

A few lines earlier this change is described as follows:

I knew that horror had paralyzed him, horror at something that was happening within him. Perhaps a vessel was breaking inside him, perhaps some poison he had long feared was at this very moment entering the chambers of his heart, perhaps a great tumor was rising in his brain like a sun that transformed the world for him.

During these same years Kafka was writing his youthful work, *Description of a Struggle,* in which he says:

What will happen to me then? Shall I be cast out from the world? . . . There is many a thing to be afraid of. That the body will vanish away, perhaps . . . that it would perhaps be well to go to church and shout aloud one's prayer, so as to draw people's looks and acquire body. . . . This fever, this seasickness on solid earth, is it not a sort of leprosy? . . . I hope to learn from you what really lies behind the things that sink down like a snowfall around me, while other people already have a little glass of schnaps standing solid as a monument on the table before them.

In direct continuation of this conversation with the supplicant in *Description of a Struggle,* Kafka wrote in his diary for 1910:

But I, of all people, feel my Ground much too often and much too strongly to be even tolerably content. I only need to feel this Ground uninterruptedly for a quarter of an hour and the poisonous world will pour into my mouth like water into a drowning man. . . . At that time, which no one can know today, for nothing can be so annihilated as that time, at that time he went wrong, when he felt his Ground all the time, just as one suddenly notices on one's body a tumor which hitherto had been the body's least thing, indeed not even the least, for so far it did not seem to exist, and which now is more than everything the body has possessed since birth. While hitherto our whole person was turned toward the work of our hands, toward the vision of our eyes, the sound in our ears, toward the steps of our feet, we now suddenly veer right round in the opposite direction, like a weathervane in the mountains. . . . The fact is, this man is no part of our people, no part of our humanity. . . . The rest of us are bound by our past and our future. . . . True, this circle belongs to us, but does so only as long as we hold it fast; no sooner do we move aside in some moment of self-oblivion . . . than we lose it at once, it slips away into space; hitherto we had kept our head down in the current of the times, now we step back, once swimmers we are now walkers, and we are lost. We are outside the law, no one knows it and yet everyone treats us accordingly.

These two passages, so strikingly similar in the very choice of images and, furthermore, written quite independently of each other during the same years by two entirely dissimilar authors, reflect the inner genesis of the great revolution in the arts that took place around 1910 and inspired both the forms of abstract painting and of modern atonal music, as well as the enigmatic hieroglyphics and hermetic imagery of, say, Georg Trakl and Franz Kafka and the late lyrics of Rainer Maria Rilke. The artists suddenly seem to take up a position outside all familiar relationships of time and space, of human discourse. They seem to abandon "the vision of our eyes, the sound in our ears," to "veer right round in the opposite direction" and to write "words" which, as

3

Rilke says, they "no longer mean," in which indeed every customary meaning "dissolves like clouds" and the "time of the different interpretation" dawns. We may recall, for example, that passage in Rilke's first Duino Elegy, of 1912, which describes a state of "being dead"—which, however, as is always the case with death in Rilke, must be incorporated into life in order "gradually to become aware of some little eternity" in the midst of "this our world":

> It is, of course, strange not to inhabit the earth any more, no longer to follow customs only just acquired, not to give the significance of a human future to roses and other things full of their own promise; no longer to be what one was in infinitely fearful hands, and to discard even one's own name like a broken toy. Strange not to go on wishing one's wishes. Strange to see adrift in space all that used to relate.

It is strange, then, to see adrift in space all that used to relate—people, things, sounds, colors, forms. Everything has lost its former familiar relationship to others and gives way to a different, unfamiliar, loose configuration of phenomena which assumes the semblance of total unrelatedness and yet demands a new interpretation of a different kind—in which, however, "not one word is left upon the other" and "all meaning dissolves."

What are we to understand by this paradoxical statement of Rilke's about an interpretation without meaning, which implies, surely, the end of all interpretation? The same paradox occurs in Kafka—in *The Trial*, for instance, where we find, in the conversation between K.

and the priest on the multiple interpretations of the parable "Before the Law," that all "opinions" about the Law, including those expressed in the novel itself, are wrong, and yet there exists one single, "unalterable scripture" of the Law. Kafka uses every means of customary logic and the most acute observation to give detailed descriptions and precise explanations of all individual phenomena and events, yet the meaning of all phenomena and explanations remains unrelievedly obscure until the end, and with every renewed attempt, interpretation literally dissolves like a cloud.

What lies at the heart of this paradox, this withdrawal from the world of people and things and their meaning? Is it a self-cancellation of man, his reality and spirit, in an extreme of hubris and despair? A declaration of man's bankruptcy, as it were? Or does it indicate the outbreak of a spiritual sickness that afflicted not merely these two writers, but perhaps the entire intellectual world of Europe, following that 1910 revolution in the arts? This interpretation is suggested by Rilke's and Kafka's strikingly identical image of the bursting tumor and the poison. But let us read the passages carefully. Kafka tells how, at the time when he constantly felt his own Ground, and at a time, furthermore, which today no one can know and which is utterly annihilated, the poisonous world entered like water into the drowning man, and how a tumor he never had before suddenly developed and caused a complete reversal and transformation in him. Rilke, too, speaks of a poison and of a tumor which suddenly burst inside him like a sun "that transformed the world for him." And a little further on we find: "It was his task to see in this horror, seemingly nothing but loathsomeness, the Being that underlies all being. There is neither choice nor refusal."

Thus for Rilke, too, the apparent outbreak of a disease is identical with awareness of an enduring Ground, of the Being that underlies all being, that is illumined as though by the sun. But why compare to a disease this attachment to the Ground, to the underlying Being beneath all being?

The texts answer this question, too. For Kafka, the man who feels his Ground all the time is a man unable to exist in a society where what counts is name, origin, money, property, and family, a man who, therefore, feels the world to be invading him like a poison. He is sharply contrasted with the man of property, who, however, is in no better case, for the loss of his possessions alone is enough to destroy him. This is clear in the lines in the diary immediately preceding those already quoted:

This, of course, is where the truth lies, the truth that can nowhere be shown so plainly. For the man who really acts the solid citizen is in no less peril, lord and master though he is, and for all that he travels the high seas in a ship, with foam before and a wake behind and much consequence all about him and is altogether different from the man weltering in the waves on his few bits of wood that, furthermore, knock one against the other and thrust each other down. For he and his property are not one, but two, and whoever breaks the connection, breaks him as well.

We and our acquaintances are quite indiscernible in this respect, because we are all covered up; I, for instance, am now covered up by my job, by my imagined and real sufferings, my literary inclinations, etc. But I, of all people, feel my Ground much too often and much too strongly. . . .

And likewise Rilke describes the individual who feels the Being that underlies all being as one "thrown away" by life and society, as a "beggar" more lost than a beggar, because he has somehow come to be excluded from all property relationships, and like a leper, cast out. In close connection with this, both writers question man's capacity for cognition and expression. "Is it possible," Rilke asks, "to have never yet seen, perceived and said anything real and important . . . to have had millennia in which to look, reflect and record, and . . . in spite of civilization, religion and philosophy, to have remained on the surface of life? . . . Yes, it is possible." The Being that underlies all being cannot, for Rilke, be expressed either by language or thought, because both at once objectify it, that is, transform it into finite relationships, plain to see and therefore superficial. An analogous idea occurs in Kafka, for instance, when he writes: "Truth is indivisible and therefore cannot perceive itself. Only the lie can perceive truth." And again: "What one is cannot be expressed, just because one is it; one can communicate only what one is not, that is, the lie." Finally, "For anything outside the world of the senses, language can be used only allusively and never even approximately for comparisons, for language, corresponding to the world of the senses, treats only of property and its relationships."

We have here a precise statement of a connection between the property order and the system of relationships in an objectified world, and the forms of human cognition and expression. Thanks to his cognition, his denomination of things, and classification of them in order and relationships, man has gained mastery over nature by transforming its immediacy of being into the mediative forms of having, naming, and possessing. There can be no doubt that this radical critique of cognition and language, which runs through the whole range of modern poetry (and is found, for instance, in Hofmannsthal, Georg Trakl, the expressionists of the Sturm group, the surrealists, and others), arises from a specifically modern experience. It is the experience of a consistently and thoroughly rationalized and objectified industrial society, in which all the soul's immediate forms of expression are sacrificed to a system of calculable and mechanized mediative relationships, which make possible and uphold domination and possession. The great change, Kafka's and Rilke's withdrawal from the world of people and things and their relationships, as well as that period's corresponding turn toward nonfigurative art, is man's protest against the dehumanization witnessed day after day in our objectified industrial society. Rilke and Kafka contracted out of that society. This becomes quite plain, for instance, on reading the beginning of Rilke's *Malte Laurids Brigge*, with its trenchant criticism of the dehumanization of urban life in Paris, or else Kafka's descriptions, almost identical in form and content, of life in a great city (for example, in his early stories *Wedding Preparations* and *Description of a Struggle*).

At the same time, both writers seem to succumb to a strange dialectic. It is precisely when they contract out of society that they seem all the more compulsively to fall under its power. The process of alienation and loss of soul that takes place objectively in industrial society finds its subjective continuation within Rilke's and Kafka's heroes themselves, whose self-alienation, indeed objectification, reaches a degree unequaled in world literature. "Like a sheet of blank paper I drifted along the houses." Further on, he writes: "And then . . . the uttermost happened: I lost all consciousness, I simply dropped out . . . and lay there like a thing among all the cloths, just like a thing." There are innumerable passages of this kind in Rilke. And Kafka writes "that at some time all the people who want to live will look like me; cut out of yellow tissue paper, just like silhouettes . . . and when they walk, one will hear them crinkle." He continues elsewhere, "Have I not, rather, a right to complain stubbornly that I skip along the houses like a shadow without proper contours, sometimes disappearing in the panes of shop windows?" The individual literally succumbs to the things and the window dressing that exemplify the commercial and fetishistic character of the products of modern industry. Subject becomes object, the alienated thing itself. But conversely, object becomes subject, the enigmatic cipher of self-alienated subjectivity, since the object itself is nothing but a man-made artificial construct. Here, at last, we are face to face with the central problem of modern poetry and art: the barrier between subject and object begins to fall. Their extreme alienation leads to their ultimate identity. No longer, as in the older poetry, does the sentient individual face a related yet clearly distinct world of described objects, so that the subject can find direct expression in the medium of nature and his social surroundings without blurring the dividing line between the two, leading to a close and intimate relationship in which, nevertheless, each sphere is left intact; no longer, therefore, are the images of poetry metaphors, similes, and symbols for what the subject feels, experiences, and means. Instead, subject and object become literally identical, which puts both beyond interpretation. For it is no longer possible now to relate or reduce this or that poetic image to any specific state of the soul or any objective datum. Instead, all of Kafka's poetic images are at once subjective and objective. They are modes of expressing a total world condition that cannot be related to anything outside itself and therefore one that cannot be interpreted, cannot be elucidated in terms of any so-called deeper significance, or of some intended other meaning, except insofar as these images disclose just that total world condition. The inner life is neither psychologically described, interpreted, nor explained as in previous narrative writing, nor does it find immediate emotional expression, as in the mood lyrics of the nineteenth century. Rather, it disappears in an objectified world. Conversely, the objective world loses its empirical spatio-temporal relationships and turns into the enigmatic hieroglyphic of an inner world that no longer means itself by its own words. A similar development could be demonstrated in the writings of Georg Trakl, Rilke, or the surrealists.

The following example may serve to illustrate this identification of the subjective with the objective, and vice versa, in Kafka:

He held his lower lip fast with his upper teeth, looked straight ahead and did not move. "Your behavior is quite senseless. Whatever has happened to you? Your business is not brilliant, but then it is not bad either; even if it were to fail, which is out of the question, you can very easily get a footing somewhere else, you are young, healthy and strong, you have your commercial training and competence, you have only yourself and your mother to look after, so really, please, do pull yourself together and explain why you have made me come here in broad daylight and why you sit there in such a state?" There was a brief pause, I sat on the windowsill and he on the chair in the middle of the room. At last he said: "All right, I'll explain it all to you. What you said was all quite true, but remember it has rained without letting up since yesterday; it was about five in the afternoon"—he looked at the time—"when it started to rain yesterday and today at four o'clock it is still raining. Surely that is enough to give one pause. And then, while it usually rains only in the street and not indoors, it seems to be the other way round this time. Look out of the window, please, it is dry down below, isn't it? There you are. But here the water is rising all the time. Let it rise, though, let it rise. It's bad, but I can bear it.

With a little good will one can bear it, one just floats a little higher on one's chair, conditions do not alter much, it is just that everything floats and one floats a little higher. But it's this beating of the raindrops on my head that I cannot bear. It seems a trifle, but it's just this trifle that I can't bear, or perhaps I might even bear that, only I can't bear having no defense against it. And I have no defense, I put on a hat, I open an umbrella, I hold a plank over my head, nothing helps, either the rain penetrates everything or else it begins to rain anew and as heavily underneath the hat, the umbrella, the plank."

This passage, a fragment from Kafka's posthumous notebooks, is particularly illuminating, since it may be regarded as an incomplete, preliminary stage in the development of Kafka's imagery, in which one can trace the genesis, as it were, of his creative style. The hero can still hold on reasonably well to the world of business, family, and so forth, yet he feels alarmed or menaced in a way incomprehensible to his companion. This state of inner spiritual crisis is expressed in the objective image of rain falling upon his head inside the room and, finally, even underneath his hat and umbrella. This image could still, on the pattern of older, traditional styles, be taken as a metaphor, as a simile for a spiritual condition. Yet it does assume strangely autonomous aspects, insofar as the image simultaneously figures a real change in the objective world—the chair floating in the room, and so on. It is, in fact, left open whether the rain pouring down on him really represents an internal menace alone or may equally be taken as a menace emanating from the objective world. In his completed works Kafka was quite consistent in making his images autonomous. The image ceases to be symbolic and assumes objective reality. In the short story, "The Metamorphosis," Gregor Samsa one morning actually does wake up as an enormous insect, and this metamorphosis is by no means treated merely as a simile, but remains to the end a real event within bourgeois society, so that subjective spiritual states and objective tangible reality merge into a completely indivisible unity. As a dreamer sees his own spiritual state in objectified images and processes and experiences them as a reality, so subjectivity is objectivized, congeals into the world of real things, with the result that in Kafka's work dream situations and reality blend indistinguishably into each other. This is in clear contrast to all the earlier dream literature of the Romantic or Baroque periods, for instance, in which despite—or perhaps just because of—all the bewildering or ironically skeptical transitions from dream to life, from life to dream, there is still a clear awareness that the two spheres are distinct.

The consequences are far-reaching and significant. Subjectivity no longer understands itself as such. "An end to psychology!" cried Kafka, and with these words broke out of the centuries-old delusion of European subjectivism that man's inner life was separated *toto genere* from the outer world and capable of being interpreted in isolation. In short, subjectivity is bodied forth in objective factualness.

But it works both ways. The objective world, the empirical world of matter, space, and time, is radically subjectivized. For insofar as the real world of space and time is a human world, it is not a world in the absolute, and it cannot be interpreted in isolation. Objectivity reveals its face only in extreme subjective experience; in the alienated, dehumanized world of our society there is no event that yields up its truth except through such experience, that is not a cipher message of human suffering. Objective society itself is marked by the features of its individual members, but not merely in the sense that subjective states can be traced in the object, but in the sense that objectivity itself is exposed only when looked at with the eyes of that selfsame extreme subjectivity that it rejects. "You need not leave the house," writes Kafka. "Stay at your table and listen. Don't even listen, just wait. Don't even wait, just be completely still and alone. The world will offer itself to you for exposure, it cannot do otherwise, it will writhe before you in ecstasy." Extreme subjectivity that contracts out of society in every way, that veers right round in the opposite direction, that steps out from the current of time and indeed out of humanity—only such subjectivity in its utter weakness has the strength to expose and make visible the objective world and its laws. For anyone who swims with the current of society cannot see through either the stream or its laws. Society can be lifted off its hinges only from the isolated Archimedean fulcrum outside society. The ordered relationships (and that means the laws) of society can be fully understood only by one who no longer thinks and acts within them. This means that the complete exposure of society's alienation process is possible only when the individual rejects the objectifying thinking that characterizes our entire modern technical and scientific world. It is just by contracting out of society altogether that Kafka's heroes discover the innermost principles of the mechanism of society, as revealed in the incisively drawn dialectical structures of Kafka's self-contradictory bureaucracies, law courts, banks, inns, schools, giant hotels, execution machines, and labyrinthine buildings. The imagery Kafka elaborates seems to be distorted by extreme subjectivism, for in empirical reality there are, strictly speaking, no such organizations. But this subjective distortion is in fact the most rigorous objectivity. For what is brought to light is exclusively and solely modern society's alienation process itself, neither veiled nor mitigated by comforting interpretations, philosophical props, historical theories, or sociological Utopias, such as are still characteristic of the so-called realistic novel. In comparison with Kafka, the realistic novel is an ideological construction, which, furthermore, by its representation of allegedly real people and conditions, allows the reader the escape of interpreting that representation as a reflection solely of some specific society and hence as not applying to himself. The fact that in Kafka's novels the organization of the powers-that-be cannot be explained is the mark of their objectivity and realism; Kafka was indeed fully justified in calling himself a mere "imitator" of reality.

This inexplicability is the catastrophe of alienated,

objectivized thought itself. The technological attempt to gain control of the world, to comprehend it, dominate it, take full possession of it, in thought and deed, exacts its price in the shape of utter ignorance of what and who is dominated. Poseidon, recording and calculating to the limit his ocean possessions, never saw nor knew his own sea. The officials, who register and judge K.'s every move, are incapable of keeping track of their own records, let alone of bearing the sight of K., which reduces them to utter impotence. Kafka's work not only breaks out of the delusion of centuries of European subjectivism that implies that the individual is capable of understanding his own psyche in nonobjective inwardness, but it also exposes the delusion of Europe's equally secular objectivism, according to which pure, nonsubjective thought can reduce the world to general principles, can fully understand and dominate it, the pure idea being identical with pure reality. Kafka's officials, in their uniform nonsubjectiveness, record and register all the events of human life and subordinate them to a general law. This gives them unlimited power, but it also puts beyond their grasp both the law, which they themselves do not know, and the very substance of real life, the human individuality that fits into no general principles. "All the authorities had to do," we read in *The Castle,* "was merely to defend remote, invisible things on behalf of remote, invisible masters, whereas K. was fighting for something living and close at hand, for himself."

Thus it becomes clear why there can be no contact between K. and the authorities, why K. literally cannot breathe the authorities' air nor they his air. The individual self, man's own being, cannot be known or formulated and recorded, for thereby the very essence of his being would be sacrificed and would become a disposable possession. Being would become having. K. resists being turned into an object for officials and their records. The officials resist the unreserved and unconditional admittance of K. because, as Bürgel says, they would thereby risk disrupting their own organization and, indeed, the completeness of the principles that govern the world. The individual cancels the general, and vice versa. And this gives us the key to the inexplicability both of K.'s struggle and of the meaning of Kafka's strange bureaucracies. Were Kafka, or rather his hero K., to formulate the meaning of his struggle and to determine the content of his desires and aims in unequivocal terms, he could indeed be helped, he could arrange his life like any other villager in the world; everything would be simple and clear. But thereby he would betray his struggle, lose his self, become, like the villagers, an "indistinguishable" instrument and object for the authorities. Kafka feels his "Ground much too strongly" to be "content" with any fixed position. K.'s struggle is more revolutionary than all the world's revolutionary struggles for power, because it is a struggle not for power but for the abolition of power, an abolition, however, which may not be defined as such, lest it be degraded into just one ideology among many, equally fixed and hence predictable.

But again it works both ways. The general law that guarantees the social and world order can likewise be neither explained nor known. The officials register all the events of life, but do not know the code of law that governs them, nor its truth. They judge events according to limited, continually shifting and contradictory points of view. "Truth is indivisible, and therefore cannot perceive itself; only the lie can perceive truth." It is as impossible to take possession of truth as of the actual, individual self. In fact, in one of Kafka's extreme dialectical reversals the general truth and the individual self become identical. "The outlaws are themselves the only law," he once wrote, and elsewhere: "Not everyone can see the truth, but he can be it." Accordingly, the officials' work is determined equally by an unknown law and by K.'s individual existence, as we see in *The Castle*: "He was by this time an adept at playing on . . . this official apparatus. On the whole, the trick consisted in doing nothing, in letting the apparatus work on its own and in merely forcing it to work by standing there, irremovable in ones earthly weight." The principles that govern the world depend upon man's simply being what he is, as in *The Trial* the individual is responsible for everything in the world, guilty of every sin, and perishes only because he does not accept this responsibility and guilt, does not recognize the law of his being, but looks for law and guilt outside himself. Similarly, in *The*

Castle, the official Bürgel indicates to K. that he himself can determine and abolish the system of authorities, that indeed the officials themselves yearn and hope for nothing so much as for such a destruction of their apparatus, which would be tantamount to a quite inconceivable promotion, to an ascent into the stratosphere of freedom.

Individuum est ineffabile. Individuality can never be subsumed in generality. It is the explosive force that not only forever compels generality to undertake new work, new records, definitions, provisions, reviews, and revisions—a process that goes on steadily not only in our humanistic and natural sciences, but also in all ideologies, philosophies, and social theories—but also forever threatens to disrupt and abolish that same generality. Conversely, generality is a threat to the individual; it tries to transform him into a subservient object and an implement. It follows that the two parties necessarily display opposing tendencies: K. makes desperate efforts to be accepted into the system of authorities, for the individual cannot exist without generality, which alone helps him to attain to self-knowledge no less than to effective existence. K. can take root and measure the land only through the intermediary of the system of authorities. Conversely, the faceless, uniformed officials can become human only through individuation. That is why they long for the disruption of their organization by the spontaneous, unannounced entry of the individual, K., in the dead of night, at a time when no official is prepared and none protected, when none has his response predetermined by an administrative rule or regulation or any ideological line of thought. But, the official Bürgel explains, such an unannounced entry is quite impossible, because every matter that the subject might wish to raise with the authorities, every request or demand or even thought to be brought before them must have been registered in advance by the officials, so that the subject "is served a writ" in his own "cause" even before he is aware of that cause, for everything that goes on in the subject is predetermined by general principles and cannot even be formulated without their intermediary. It could, therefore, be "proved" that there was "no room in this world" for spontaneity and freedom. "Thus the world corrects its own course and keeps in equilibrium. It is a splendid, continuously and unimaginably splendid arrangement, though from another point of view utterly bleak."

While K. thus continually objectivizes himself—necessarily so, since he is a thinking subject—he again and again succumbs to the mechanism of society, is identified with it, becomes an element and object of its apparatus, against which he nonetheless tries to assert his unfathomable—and therefore free—self. The latter, in its turn, is identical with the general law of any moral world order, resting, as any morality must, upon freedom of the will—a law, moreover, which ultimately governs the officials who do not know and cannot define it, because it would thereby cease being determined by freedom.

The dialectic is permanent and incalculable, as is shown in the ceaseless dialectical reflections and the dialectically forever changing action and imagery of Kafka's works. Insofar as subject and object seek to assume concrete reality, they prove identical precisely in their lethal alienation. What comes to pass inside, happens outside; outside events are inwards, just as the power of Klamm, the official, is manifest at the most intimate place of all, in K.'s bedroom.

The relentlessly consistent dialectical form of Kafka's writing exposes centuries-old spiritual and social struggles. In these longstanding conflicts subjective criticism of society and objective oppression, individual and community, feeling and reason, freedom and terrorism, progress and reaction were played off against each other in the limiting theses of their time. Kafka shows them to be what they always were, namely, identical theses in which freedom always turned into terrorism and progress into reaction to fortify, paradoxically, the very structures of human domination against which the progressives fought. Kafka refused to formulate in his work any kind of limited historical, sociological, or philosophical position. He hermetically sealed off his work against any concrete relationship with time and history, and he seemingly produced nothing but unreal, spectral fictions. By these means he succeeded in developing the dialectic at the heart of human history, in creating an awareness of the "truth" which, as Kafka once said, is hidden in the chorus of all lies. If Kafka's work seems unintelligible and indeed impenetrable, this does not stem from any mystical irrationality or renunciation of knowledge, both of which are ruled out by the sheer logic and concentration of his language. It is, rather, an expression of a *transcending* awareness that avoids any sort of restrictive statement, rejects any consolation that reinforces delusion, and criticizes the world as well as itself in order to reach the *whole* truth.

> In the struggle between yourself and the world, support the world. No one must be cheated, nor the world of its victory. . . . The spirit becomes free only when it ceases to be a prop. . . . Is it possible to think anything disconsolate? Or rather, anything disconsolate without a glimmer of consolation? It might be a way out that insight as such is consolation. . . . Forward only, oh hungry animal, lies the road to eatable food, to breathable air and free life, even if it should be beyond life. And who gives you the strength? Whoever gives you clarity of vision.

Kafka's ultimate aim is freedom. It is reached only through insight, but an insight that goes so far as to demolish even its own objectivizations and only for this reason appears impenetrable, for every explanatory thesis must be revoked and replaced by others in order to reach the utmost possible completeness, the whole truth. For "in the chorus of all lies there may be a deal of truth," says Kafka. He gains a full view only by stepping out of the current of time, as it were, so that the world, alienated, appears to him entirely different from what it is to those in the midst of the current, and this is how Kafka's seemingly untransparent world ultimately makes the world transparent. Alienation serves insight.

Kafka's concept of truth and existence must, therefore, also be strictly distinguished from any kind of metaphysical, ontological, or existentialist interpretation. Kafka's "indivisible truth" or individual "self" is the very essence of all human experience and, indeed, all human thought; it is not anything prior to, underlying, or beyond experience and thought, let alone accessible through intuitive and irrational soul searching. In 1911 Kafka wrote: "No self-knowledge should ever be regarded as final enough for writing down before it is fully complete with all incidental consequences, and utterly truthful." Kafka's criticism of rationally objectivizing thought is not directed against that kind of thought itself, without which human existence is inconceivable. Rilke looked in the here and now for a paradoxical immediacy, beyond thought, of what is mediated; thus, despite all the similarities between his and Kafka's positions around 1910, he took quite a different path. Kafka expanded and intensified rational thought to the point of repeatedly trying to explode his own limiting objectivizations by the optimal use of all the potentialities of thought to gain full understanding and freedom. Here, too, dialectic is at work. The quantitative increase in rationally and logically objectivizing thought destroys all the objectivizations themselves in turn, and leads to a qualitatively new kind of thought that generates freedom through the ceaseless destruction of objectivizations. "The spirit becomes free only when it ceases to be a prop." Only thus can we explain the strange statement that there may be a deal of truth in the chorus of all theses, errors, and lies. Only thus, too, can we understand the concluding sentence of Kafka's late work, "Investigations of a Dog," in which he wrote that he was concerned with a "different science" from that "practiced nowadays, an ultimate science which puts freedom above all else."

And here, too, lies the answer to the key problem in any interpretation of Kafka's work, the problem, that is, of the place of this freedom in the relentlessly consistent dialectical form of his writing. To all appearances, Kafka's permanent dialectic becomes a compulsive mechanism in which again and again the individual's free self gets caught along with society, so that Kafka's heroes have to suffer as they make their way through the bleakly persistent, wearisome monotony of labyrinthine contradictions, without ever an end in sight, let alone a positive solution or even a ray of hope. One is tempted to conclude that Kafka is describing the nihilistic final state, or the crisis, of a society which has lost all faith in absolute truth and all capacity for meaningful forms of living in this world.

Analysis has shown this conclusion to be wrong. Kafka's dialectic plainly keeps the decisive authority out of the compulsive mechanism, the authority, that is, of the free self or truth, sometimes called the "unalterable" or "undeceiving" law, which can be neither reached nor represented by any finite interpretation or form of life. He criticizes any attempt at conceiving this free self or unalterable truth in finite terms or turning it into an objective truth that could be possessed or represented. The officials who represent the absolute and unalterable law are by the very fact of representing it turned into a terroristic organization of power, or, one might say, a lay theocracy. For this sole reason absolute truth is no longer named, indeed is stated to be unrecognizable, "beyond the reach of human judgment," as Kafka says in *The Trial*. But the free self that tries to hold its own against this organization is, in its turn, put in the wrong by its very attempt to do so. For it thus fails to recognize its universal responsibility for the state of the world; it directs its criticism exclusively at the world and not at itself (*The Trial*). This means that it unilaterally hardens its own position and thereby loses its absolute freedom, transforms it into conditional freedom, and thereby inevitably succumbs to the dialectic portrayed and becomes dependent, an object of the world. K.'s downfall in *The Trial* is a consequence of that delusion, which leads the subject to defend his own rights without also acknowledging the rights of his opponent, without knowing the law which guarantees the moral order of the world and, as has been shown, is anchored in himself as the free law of moral responsibility for everything that happens. This ignorance of the law is explicitly named as his real guilt.

Kafka's criticism, therefore, is directed both against what is currently called individualism and against collectivist power systems. Strictly speaking, it is not only criticism, but a precise description of empirical reality, in which the rights and wrongs of both positions necessarily intertwine in the manner described, neither being quite right and neither quite wrong, so that in fact we get an inextricably recurring alternation of antinomies, regardless of the society or the individual under consideration. Kafka's novels are, so to speak, models of human reality, wherever and whenever it may manifest itself. In a letter to Oskar Baum, Kafka described the growth of bureaucracy as "necessary and inevitable," as an outcome of "the origin of human nature." That growth is rooted in the very nature of man, who reduces everything to rational and finite terms. But, since man is also free, he rebels against himself in his other guise. The monotony with which Kafka's heroes and bureaucracies are trapped in their antinomies is the monotony of faithful adherence to reality and its truth. If Kafka were to bring consolation into this reality by stressing and thus transfiguring any given form of life or manner of existence, he would, in the words of *The Trial*, make "the lie the order of the world."

The only consolation known to Kafka is "insight as such." It is the insight of one who no longer compromises—and none other can have insight; the insight of a man bereft of power, an outsider, who indeed can use his insight against himself. Only such a man can draw a faithful picture of the world, only he can expose the world by representing it. To condemn such a mirror is to condemn oneself. For no one is free from the lie who cannot face the mirror of truth. Truth and freedom appear when the world, stripped of appearances, gives up its reality. Kafka's work is the end of all ideologies, but also the possible beginning of a world that achieves reconciliation by giving up its own antinomic theses. "I am an end or a beginning," Kafka wrote. The end may become a beginning. For this end is knowledge. And only in knowledge can there be reconciliation. The vicious circle of dialectic can be broken only when man can see through the dialectic itself. The hardening of opposite positions and the resulting intolerance and inhumanity will give way to humane patterns of life only when both positions ceaselessly correct each other in a critical protest against the chains with which mankind has fettered itself.

2

The Revolution
in Literature:
1910-1925

The revolution in the arts that took place between 1910 and 1925 and extended to every field of artistic endeavor—to music, painting, sculpture, architecture, the dance, the theatre, and literature—in German writing looks at first glance like a chaotic muddle of the most diverse tendencies, emotions, ideas, and forms of expression. There seems to be no common unifying element, except possibly in negation, in a break with tradition. But even that is not correct. There was a link with tradition, not only with the world of the so-called primitives at the dawn of history and outside written history, but also with earlier and by now historical revolutions in literature, with the *Sturm und Drang*, with Hamann, Herder, the young Goethe, with the mystical, visionary world of the Romantics, with the political activism of the Young Germany movement and its ecstatically rationalist confidence in the power of reason and progress, and also with the so-called "Gothic man" of the Middle Ages.

Utterly irreconcilable elements entered into the 1910–1925 revolution in literature that seem to give it the aspect of an impenetrable confusion of conflicting forces. It cannot even be fittingly described by the generic term "Expressionism." Not only was the concept of Expressionism defined in entirely different ways in the course of this literary revolution, but "Expressionism" as such was explicitly and sharply attacked in numerous manifestoes, which themselves were a significant part of the 1910–1925 revolutionary movement in literature.

It even seems that the characteristic of this revolution was its obliteration of all characteristics and its deliberate production of a flood of mutually contradictory "isms," ending up with the "program of no programs" (W. Michel), with the satirical negation of any definable position and message (S. Friedlaender, Dadaism, etc.).

This very fact, however, enables the observer looking back from today's vantage point to discern that movement's common ground and outlook. For the first time in the history of artistic revolutions, an attempt was made to put under a microscope as many as possible of the elements and prerequisites of artistic creation, to define them experimentally through analysis and synthesis, to test them out in every imaginable and usable means of expression, and to translate them into artistic production. In all this the words "elements and prerequisites" are to be understood in the most comprehensive sense. They include not only the artist's media, such as words, sounds, colors, lines, and so on, which acquire autonomous and absolute expressive qualities, but also the whole nature of man, that is to say, the elements and prerequisites of his physical, spiritual, and intellectual world. These too were isolated in "pure" form, were "disengaged" from their spatial, temporal, historical, and sociological contexts and in this sense made "absolute," thus opening up an endless play of new possibilities, combinations, and "syntheses." Naturally enough, there emerged juxtapositions and oppositions of such absolute elements. The "experience" in itself, the pure "immediacy" of physical and spiritual sensation, became the program of the *Sturm* circle, with all its irrationalist and formal consequences, such as the disruption of all preestablished conventions of language—for example, syntax, historical etymology, meter, strophe pattern, and so forth, so as to allow the spontaneous experience to pass directly into absolute expression in "sound, rhythm and image." The Activists, on the other hand, based their counterprogram on "pure reason," the mind as such, sacrificing the "soul," "dull inwardness," the uncontrollable "experience" and its "expression." In this way they were also breaking up all social order and disorder so as to prepare the way for the absolute realm of peace governed by reason, the higher—indeed highest—"ecstatically" activist reason that was to prevail. Pure "movement," leaving space and time behind and advancing into the absolute with the help of technology, became the torch of the Futurists. The cost was the sacrifice of all traditions, and the risk the approval of every kind of war, violence, and barbarism for the sake of technical progress and the absolute release of industrial man. The complete realization of the solipsistic "personality," freely living out its own self, was the idea behind Carl Sternheim's mordant social satires, whereas Georg Kaiser heralded the "birth of the new man" through an escape from industrial society, and at the same time a vision of religious, ecstatic rebirth through humility and renunciation was put forward by R. J. Sorge, Franz Werfel, Lothar Schreyer, and others.

And finally, all these atomized "absolute" elements of man and his art were emptied of their content in Dadaism. The absolutes themselves were again made relative, but no longer with reference to any overriding meaning and context; instead, they were carried ad absurdum in playful satire that offered new juxtapositions of all the elements of language and existence. As the atomization of language, of pictorial subjects, of social phenomena, and so on, entered into the themes and forms of Dadaist art, a weirdly gay court of justice—without-judges was in session, and an "indifferent Zero" became manifest in which the revolution in literature, as it were, saw through itself and came to a stop.

The historical origin and the significance of this release of the elements of man's art and existence may be understood and explained, in the first place, as a protest and revolt against the increasing collectivization and relativization of man in the latter part of the nineteenth and the beginning of the twentieth century. This has, in fact, frequently been stated, partly in the very programs and declarations of this revolution in literature. Psychology, biology, and sociology, so the argument runs, as well as the naturalist and impressionist trends in art, had integrated man into a complicated network of hereditary and environmental factors, had caused him to become the "product" of general principles definable in social, scientific, or medico-psychiatric terms. Man and his expression in art had become mere reflections or results of overriding historical, psychological, or sociological processes. Art had meaning only in relation to history, society, and civilization. Growing industrialization and specialization had turned man into an impotent link in an all-powerful social apparatus. In view of this situation, the argument continues, revolutionary art after 1910 sought the "absolute" representation of "absolute" values and of man's absolute, indestructible elemental forces. Art was no longer to take as its "subject" the changing contents of the soul's experiences; instead, the soul itself and its experience were to be captured directly and absolutely in word, color, and sound. The confusing abundance of the mind's possible reflections, with all its skeptical, relativist implications, was no longer to be "imitated," but the mind itself, as an active, postulating force establishing absolute values, was to exert a direct, revolutionary influence on the age and to set an unconditional and inalienable goal for the future. What was in question was no longer the incidental "use" or "harm" of mechanized labor, but technology in the absolute, intensified to the point of completely releasing man from the bonds of time and space (Futurism).

The protest against the collectivization and specialization of man can, therefore, take the form of either a revolt of the "soul" and "love" against technology, as in Ernst Toller's *The Machine Wreckers,* or else of an unconditional endorsement of technology with a view to its total mastery over nature as well as the complete liberation of man and his independence in practice.

To postulate man's elements and aims as absolute in this manner may be considered—as Georg Lukács has in his analyses of Expressionism—a Utopian disregard of "reality," and hence this revolution may be accused of having not been a true "revolution," but merely an excursion into fantasy and unreality. As such, it can be said to have contained no threat to the enduring and ever growing social forces of enslavement, but on the contrary to have played into their hands, for these revolutionaries' impotent protest was carried to the point of absurdity, and thus it indirectly justified the "reactionary" forces in leaving everything unchanged or in blindly developing further along "realistic" lines.

But, strangely, on closer examination those who criticize the literary revolution of 1910 on these grounds are seen to judge it by the same standards as their reactionary opponents. Both reactionary bourgeois society and the progressive revolutionary social critics criticized this literary revolution from a "realistic" standpoint, however much the intellectual and factual structures of their realism may have differed and indeed clashed, and even though, as Georg Lukács has rightly argued, bourgeois realism may have been concealed in a naive, ideological disguise by means of those selfsame Utopian and unreal features that emerged in Expressionism, Activism, and the rest. Arguments based on man's "inwardness," on his "soul," on the "rebirth" and "renewal" of man have at all times provided bourgeois society with the ideological justification for its crimes and its allegedly revivifying "baths of steel"—witness the war poems of leading bourgeois poets in 1914. But in penetrating this ideological disguise of the actual, realistic bourgeois will to power, in exposing the contradictions of economic and historical development and the step-by-step revolutionizing of realistic transformation of human society, "progressive" social realism became the agent of that very collectivization and divisive specialization that were the mark of bourgeois society's capitalistic realism, against which Karl Marx had rebelled in the nineteenth century in the same way as the 1910 revolution rebelled in literature.

The crucial question was this: can a positive social revolution be accomplished by an exclusively "realistic" approach? That is to say, can it be accomplished by the exclusion of everything Utopian which, as Alfred Döblin once expressed it in "Wissen und Verändern," is mere burdensome baggage to be removed from the cannonading, armored train of history only at the end of the contradictory historical process, in a classless society free of contradictions, when Utopia can become reality?

It is only in the light of this question that the Utopian manifestoes of the 1910–1925 revolution in literature acquire their historical and supra-historical significance. Amid the maze of contradictions of twentieth-century history, these manifestoes proclaimed their critical exposures as well as their prophetic promise of what man, without knowing it, really is and what he could and should become. Insofar as this revolution in the arts cut through to the elements of man and his art, it performed two functions proper to every genuinely revolutionary attitude, namely, critical exposure and positive guidance. The harsh, distorted pictures executed by the Futurists, Cubists, Expressionists, and others shattered not merely the harmonious lies of an objectively represented "sound" world, but also displayed the intellectual and spiritual powers of expression that both claim and warrant a free existence worthy of man. To make an absolute of the spirit, the soul, the free personality, and so on was not an illusionist concealment of an evil world that, behind the mask of big words and gestures, pursued its real business and barbarities quite undisturbed. If this contention of Lukács's were correct, the works of these artists would not have been banned and burned as "degenerate." Their revolutionary impulse was instinctively grasped by a reactionary and fascist society better than it was by the later socialist realism, which in its fight against this revolution in the arts was and remains a traitor to its own origins.

The release of the "elements" of man performed the revolutionary task of making visible critical postulates by which society could be judged and altered. It is in the nature of every critical postulate to be unreal and Utopian. That does not nullify the unconditional character of its claim, but on the contrary justifies and confirms it. The more unconditional, absolute, that is, "unreal," is its claim, the more powerful is its challenging effect. To postpone it to the end of history is to destroy it and smooth the way to unlimited barbarism and the realistic enslavement of man.

But this implies, too, that the seemingly nihilistic turn this revolution in the arts took in Dadaism, for instance, acquires a new and different kind of meaning. To Dadaism belongs the enduring historic merit of having seen through and invalidated the dialectic of every Utopia with a prescribed content. Every Utopia that takes as absolute any of man's specific spheres, elements, or demands leads to the tyranny of these spheres, elements, and demands over other powers and potentialities equally present in man. This was the deeper anthropological cause of the historical fact, described earlier, that in this revolution in the arts the most varied Utopias and absolutes arose in juxtaposition and opposition to each other. The seeming chaos of conflicting tendencies stemmed from an inner necessity of this revolutionary process. The disruption of bourgeois relativism, the drive to unconditional postulates and art forms, was bound to lead to this multiplicity of "absolute" art forms and modes of thought. But in Dadaism the absolute is deprived of any kind of definable content. Only thus, however, does the absolute become truly absolute, disengaged from every relation. To equate the absolute and nothingness is one of mankind's old, old ideas, one that recurs time and again in the history of metaphysics from Buddha to Hegel. The Dadaists, S. Friedlaender, and other representatives of this literary revolution in their turn picked up this idea and developed it meaningfully insofar as they subjected to criticism every expression of life and art, whether given or, as to its content, postulated. This criticism could, in the nature of things, take only negative form, for it had no standard left by which to measure. But it took a seriously positive line with the equally old demand that man should give free play to all his powers and potentialities, for only then does he fully enter into man's estate. It was not without reason that Dadaism gave rise to surrealist art that attempted to represent all man's subconscious and semi-conscious worlds in order to bring into view the total reality of human existence.

Although Dadaism thus nullified all postulates of fixed content, its seeming nihilism aimed at the universal self-realization of man. This becomes completely clear if we examine, for instance, the religious background of the ideas of the Dadaist Hugo Ball.

It follows that we must take a new and different look at the place of this revolution in the history of European art. It was not a reaction against Naturalism, Impressionism, and the rest, but an extension of art forms and aims long since introduced and developed by European art in the nineteenth and early twentieth century. The French Impressionists and Symbolists had, as Hugo Friedrich pointed out in *Die Struktur der modernen Lyrik*, evolved their revolutionary new art forms and language under the sign of an "absolute" world disengaged from all relations, a world of "empty transcendence," in Hugo Friedrich's words. Even then the idea was the same: against the objectified, banal world produced by modern industrialization, the work of art was to establish an indomitable world safe from any encroachments. So-called modern art started later in Germany than in France because it was only after the great burst of company promotions in 1870–1871 that industrialization led to provincial decline and to metropolitan concentration on the scale reached by Paris in the middle of the nineteenth century, during the Second Empire. Consequently, Naturalism and Symbolism first appeared in German art in the years between 1880 and 1890. The two movements were nothing but hostile brothers, as they had been in France. They developed simultaneously in both cases—the Goncourt brothers alongside Mallarmé, Gerhart Hauptmann alongside Stefan George and Hofmannsthal. And a look at their essential aims reveals fundamentally analogous purposes. The young Stefan George, influenced by the French Symbolists, created in his *Algabal* an absolute world outside time and space, in which even the laws of nature, of the seasons, and of organic life were no longer valid. What Arno Holz, the founder of so-called consistent Naturalism, had in mind with his formula, "Art tends to return to nature," was a "nature" that comprised the entire physical, spiritual, and intellectual life of man and contained within itself an unattainable transcendence. What he wanted was not at all a photographic copy of external nature, but the representation of the world "behind all things," the "ultimate of all ultimates." And in matters of form he anticipated the aesthetic theory and practice of the Expressionist artists of the *Sturm* group, in that like them he established and taught a "verbal" art that sought to enclose the immediate "experience" itself within a form of words appropriate to it in rhythm, sound, and image, while at the same time breaking up all conventional word formations and disregarding all established aesthetic rules in such matters as meter, strophe pattern, and rhyme. The central problem of Arno Holz's theory of poetry and of his own poetic creation was that of the inherent laws of the particular medium, of words, sounds, colors, lines, and so on.

In this perspective, the 1910–1925 revolution in the

arts appears as a great wave in the vaster tide of modern art. The distinguishing mark of this tide is that in an age that degraded thought itself and reduced every so-called philosophy of life to mere objects of practical interest, art undertook the task of creating a world that could neither be dominated nor made amenable to any purpose. But the meaning and aim of bygone classical art were no different; what was behind Schiller's idea of "free play" was no different either. And this play was for Schiller, the "classic," a matter of revolutionary seriousness. Witness the prologue to *The Bride of Messina*: "The purpose of genuine art is not a mere passing show; it seeks in earnest not just to give man a momentary illusion of freedom, but to set him truly and really free."

Thus, at bottom, the 1910–1925 revolution in the arts sought merely to fulfill the mission of all art, namely, the liberation of man. Its forms were more radical, its programs more extreme than those of earlier art. But society's methods of enslavement, too, had become more extreme. Schiller's idea of freedom itself had become the prototype of this society with its "humane" enslavement. Art was left with no vestige of any ideology. It had no option but to become abstract or else contemptuously to smash all prototypes. Art is not the mirror of its age, but its antagonist. It may not naively and uncritically reflect an image of its time. The mission of art is fulfilled only in the vision of what man as a whole can and should be, that is to say, only in Utopia.

3

Franz Kafka:
A Portrait

Franz Kafka's work is the purest literary expression of the twentieth century, but for that very reason it is the most inaccessible to those involved in this epoch. His work reflects the world in a state in which it "has not yet found its way into our consciousness."[1] Everyone senses this; hence, the writer's worldwide fame. But no one else has overstepped the traditional bounds of consciousness; hence, the bewilderment he arouses. All the other writers of the present epoch, even Thomas Mann, Robert Musil, Hermann Broch, James Joyce, and Marcel Proust, directly reflect the state of consciousness of our age, including its subconscious strata. But Kafka re-creates the world from a point of view situated "outside our humanity."[2] He refused to allow himself to be swept along by the current of the life and consciousness of his time; he "steps back" from the "current of the times" and "sees different things and more than others; he is, after all, dead in his own lifetime and yet the real survivor."[3]

Inevitably the work of someone who has thus crossed the periphery of life assumes alien and incomprehensible forms and content. Reality, as it were, bursts into his work unfiltered, unsoftened, unguided by preestablished modes of thought and perception. No regulative power is left, in Kafka's work, even to the spatio-temporal modes of perception that unalterably predetermine our human experience and establish a generally accepted human system of values, for these modes of perception are far outstripped by human reality. A whole lifetime may not be enough to reach what is merely "closest at hand," yet the most distant moment can be attained in a flash. Thus, in Kafka's work, time and space may contract or expand according to the total human reality which encompasses them. (See *The Country Doctor*, a collection of fourteen tales.) It is of the essence that Kafka does not justify these changes in the normal correlations of time and space in terms either of our subjective sense of time and space, or of the scientific theory of relativity, or of our imagination's ability to associate at will the relations of time and space. Rather, he sees these changes as inevitably arising out of the structure of man. What is close at hand for man may in reality be most remote, and vice versa. There is no end to the discrepancies between consciousness and truth. A man's conceptions in any given case by no means correspond to its truth, which is out of his reach, yet lies within himself. The paradoxes of this state of affairs fundamentally determine the themes and the form of Kafka's writing.

Man is no longer portrayed in the perspective of his own ways of living, perceiving, and thinking, but in the setting of the contradictions inherent in his total existence. As a result, there is no longer any need for certain principles that had hitherto governed the form and content of narrative writing. It is not merely that the modes of spatio-temporal conception that safeguard and regulate the world of our experience are abandoned and transformed. In addition, the mental forms and contents by which we motivate, justify, and interpret our emotional and intellectual life are exposed and relinquished as inadequate, deceptive principles which, by misrepresenting and distorting the fullness of human reality, establish a mere pseudo-system of values. Accordingly, the characters of Kafka's novels and stories are not constructed and guided by anything explicitly formulated— be it views or philosophies of life, spiritual ideas, aims or demands, impulses of the will, feelings or psychological principles, qualities of character, or stages of development. The reader of Kafka's novels does not know what the heroes are talking about, what they want, think, feel, or aspire to—or what, for instance, the meaning is of "the struggle" that K. carries on against the castle authorities, or what K. is struggling for, or why he has to take up the struggle. In fact, the reader does not even know in what world the heroes of these novels really live. For the social order, the bureaucracies, the law courts of Kafka's fiction are completely unfathomable, undecipherable, indefinable, and cannot be understood in terms of the categories of our normal consciousness. The world seems to be out of joint. Every rule of human feeling, thinking, and acting seems to have dwindled away, every mental and spatio-temporal system of orientation to have vanished. It is as though the world of Western civilization were blotted out; in fact, it is as though the historical and natural world of man simply no longer existed. In Kafka's novels and stories the action is hermetically sealed off from the whole of history and nature. Not a sound from the world of historical mans spirit, emotion, or thought, not a breath of air from the life of "natural" man ever penetrates the labyrinths of Kafka's fictional world. Kafka denies himself even "expression" of the soul, that last inheritance of extreme loneliness, and he attains poetic beauty of expression solely through the language of legal and official records.

"I am an end or a beginning," Kafka once wrote.[4] His work is the terminus of European literary and intellectual tradition, a terminus where that tradition nullifies itself. Today there is no intellectual testimony that maintains its full validity, no culture able to shape our reality, no faith that is truly held and able to move mountains, no exemplary way of living, no authority that guarantees order. Kafka merely draws the conclusions from a development that is familiar to everyone and from a truth known to all, but repeatedly denied. His decision—to step back from "humanity's" circle of life and consciousness—originated in a European historical situation and gave that situation its most valid, because most truthful, literary expression.

But is his work also a "beginning"? The answer to this can be found only in the action within his works, impenetrable as his narrative may be at first sight. If it is true that Kafka expresses human reality itself, unsoftened and unguided by the limited, invalidated modes of thought and perception governing our present historical and natural consciousness, then we are faced with the insistent question of what constitutes human reality in Kafka, how it manifests itself, and what consequences knowledge of it entails for our contemporary life and consciousness.

It was by remarkable transpositions that Kafka, in a manner peculiar to him alone, managed to solve the difficult problem of how to capture human reality and to represent it adequately and truthfully in literature. In his work, above all in that of his mature period, the totality of human life and consciousness appears in the shape of a gigantic, infinitely elaborate, endlessly ramified and articulated system of officialdom, one that ceaselessly, "in a tearing hurry," at one and the same time notes, records, processes, and defines everything that can be lived, thought, felt, or done.

This system mirrors the present state of the world, the growing control and collectivization of every vital impulse and thought in the name of a superior knowledge of the structures of human living and thinking. Man as Homo sapiens is continuously foreseeing, feeling, remembering, and thinking, and his every experience is at the same time something consciously or subconsciously felt, imagined, or reflected upon. This is why the image of an officialdom forever registering every movement of life or consciousness corresponds to man's actual living process, to the uninterrupted transformation of Being into consciousness and of consciousness into Being, or more precisely, to the way both inseparably interlock in man's actual life. The inhuman rationalization expressed by this official filing system is an inevitable product of Homo sapiens himself. But this rationalization—and here Kafka prophetically touches the very heart of the evil—in its turn takes the form of an unconscious, irrational act executed in a state of unawareness. The officials carry out their planning, controlling, and organizing work during their sleep, or when eating, in the absence of any vital reflexes or even of consciousness, and they work the more smoothly and quickly the more tired and sleepy they are. Rationalization is thus seen as a blind, irrational process—which means that the control and collectivization of man takes place under conditions and with consequences not clear to the controllers themselves. They both know and do not know. Their control abolishes consciousness. For the more unconscious the control, the more it becomes unshakeable and insuperable. "K. thought of his [the official Klamm's] remoteness, of his impregnable dwelling, of his silence maybe interrupted only by screams such as K. had never heard, of his deep, piercing look never to be either proved or disproved, of the orbits which he described above according to incomprehensible laws and which, from K.'s own depths, could not be destroyed."[5] Silence and screams. The planning control releases from within itself uncontrollable brutality. Klamm's servants burst upon the villagers like an unbridled horde of savages, with the violence of an unleashed natural catastrophe. Unconscious rationality and planned barbarism turn out to be identical. For barbarism, too, is manipulated according to plan, as a monotonous, ever recurrent event. The villagers "took it for granted like a familiar natural occurrence and . . . seeking support in numbers, they yielded to the current."[6] The control becomes "nature," becomes "familiar," something which by continual repetition acquires the semblance of good and right and thus tacitly does away with all resistance. The villagers, who have become a "mass," accept the controlling authorities as obviously natural, as something that it would be a "crime" to resist, tantamount to a "disgrace" never to be wiped out. (See the Amalia episode in *The Castle*.) In their eyes, in fact, the collectivizing powers take on the shape of greatness, admirable and godlike. And not only in their eyes. Kafka's contemporary commentators have understood these officials in just the same way. Obscure social phenomena are objectivized as mythical powers of fate. The elimination of history reveals itself as a leap into the monotony of perpetual sameness, as the loss of free consciousness. Collectivization leads to unhistorical myth, since society interprets itself as nature and contemptuously demonstrates the superiority of "existence" over mind.

Nature and myth are the fictions that an unconsciously and irrationally planning and organizing society continually produces and reproduces in order to keep alive. Dazzled by them, those caught up in this society close their eyes to the anarchic chaos that really dwells within them. The contradictions are no longer seen as contradictions. The absurd, perpetually contradictory commands of the authorities are accepted and obeyed by the villagers without complaint as obvious and "natural" instructions. Moral action is punished as a crime, free thinking is proscribed as a "disturbance." "Officialdom and life had exchanged places."[7] Officialdom makes itself out to be the mediator of life, whereas life is completely officialized. In fact, the organization becomes a "world order" that does not suffer any other territory to exist. The power of these officials extends not only to the organization of the externals of life, but penetrates to the inmost recesses of man himself. It reflects and registers everything that can be thought, felt, perceived, or foreseen by man. Klamm's power, for instance, is at its greatest in the most intimate, most personal concerns of love, in K.'s "bedroom." That is to say, officialdom is an image of the whole biological, spiritual, intellectual, and social reality of man. It is the registry that every day goes through the Being and consciousness of all of us, to which we are in bondage and serfdom without knowing it, from which we cannot break away without destroying ourselves, just as in *The Trial* the court is "everywhere," in every place to which Josef K. "happens" to go. Knowing, we do not know. In consciousness we are unconscious, just like the officials who make their records as they sleep. And just like them we pass over our own contradictions, as though they did not exist.

Kafka's work is also a description of the inmost processes of our life and consciousness, every movement of which it reflects precisely. Human life is lived according to the limited processes of consciousnesss, to which it is unsuspectingly surrendered. We subordinate our life to aims, wishes, hopes, and views that shape and control it during and as we live it (and began before we were born), so that "free" life can no longer come into existence. We live according to prefashioned norms of our consciousness conditioned by history and "nature," and these norms cannot afterward be broken by that consciousness, with the result that they appear self-evident and natural. Consciousness becomes unconscious, transforms itself by its own spell into immediate "life." Just as the painter Titorelli in *The Trial* always paints the same picture, so life is always subsumed in the same model. It becomes a standard product. But life does not fit the model, and one model is opposed to another. From contrasting points of view the same event, the same person, can be interpreted and experienced in entirely different ways. Life is modelled on a chaos of contradictions. What consolidates life, brings order into it, is in fact the consolidation of anarchy, the justification of permanent chaos. What is more, each individual model contains internal contradictions. No one acts according to his own model, which represents the opposite of what it is. What we do does not correspond to what we think, nor does our life correspond to our beliefs. The moral principles that we pretend to follow are never obeyed in practice. What does govern our life is the vanished code of law that mankind imagines has been superseded since time immemorial. "Emperors long dead are enthroned in our villages . . . the battles of our most ancient history are fought only now . . . their misdeeds are committed all over again . . . thus the people deal with past rulers, but relegate the present ones to the dead."[8]

We strive for aims that in truth we do not want at all. " 'The plea is rejected. You may go.' An undeniable feeling of relief swept through the crowd. . . . What is so strange is that there seems no way of managing without this refusal."[9] To live up to our own moral principles would make life impossible. Ideals, in the general view, are unrealizable. They are sacrificed with "relief" in order to "manage." Kafka's absurd world reflects the logic of our lives.

Whoever defies this logic is ostracized, though not explicitly, not by decree or violence. Silently the ground is cut from under his feet, as happens to Amalia, who "saw to the bottom of it all" and "took her stand face to face with truth." All that remains to her is to "keep silent," to live "completely without hope,"[10] disowned and outcast. She may not break her "silence," for if she were to talk, she would again succumb to the "lie," just like K., who courts defeat at the hands of the authorities precisely by the spoken protest with which he "fights" them. The critic is part of the absurd system he criticizes, so long as he tries to live within it. The weapons of his criticism recoil against him. K. does indeed perceive the contradictions of life's registry, but he does not "see through" them, does not see "to the bottom" of them, because he wishes to survey the land within the existing system, looks for "connection" or "integration," or, like Josef K. in *The Trial,* wants to "reform," to "improve" the authorities by means that are rooted in the nature of the authorities themselves and therefore can alter nothing. The critic of civilization merely confirms the civilization he criticizes. As the law court usher says to Josef K. "It's quite natural to rebel."[11] Rebellion itself turns into a monotonously repeated manipulation of civilization. It expresses only what is known anyway. Although it strives for change, its gloomy doomsday images merely consolidate the fatalism of a civilization that recognizes and masochistically gloats over its own malaise in these images, and applauds the critic, only to leave everything as it is, for one just can't "manage" without it.

It is characteristic of the critic K., as of all modern critics of civilization, to look for "help" and "information" from every source, from women, lawyers, artists, teachers, and priests. He deploys all the vital and intellectual resources of modern civilization in order to discover its secret. But for him, caught as he is in the vicious circle of this civilization itself, the secret only deepens, and K. becomes more and more a prisoner of the world that he set out to "fight." "The spirit becomes free only when it ceases to be a prop,"[12] Kafka once wrote. All the "solutions" of the "crisis," which promise support and hope, reinforce the spirit's servitude. To be "face to face with truth" means to live "completely without hope." The man "dead in his own lifetime" is the "real survivor."

This is the crucial problem of Kafka's work. In that work truth is attainable only at a point "outside our humanity," because it is only from such a vantage point that the totality of human life can be seen and looked through to the bottom. Such a vantage point presupposes self-cancellation of life in the midst of life, being dead in one's own lifetime. Our historical and natural consciousness cannot follow Kafka into this paradox. Yet it is not a supernatural, mystical paradox, but a moral demand inherent in the human spirit, and one that can be fulfilled anywhere at any time. It is, in Kafka's words, the "miracle" always present in "ordinary" human life. It comes to pass in the "unguarded moment" when man, neither controlled nor guided by rigid patterns of life and thought, "virtually disrupts the official organization"[13] and "ascends into the stratosphere of freedom."[14] In one way it is an utterly unpremeditated moment of matter-of-course, silent self-sacrifice when the mother, in the short story "The Married Couple," revives her dead husband by the simple, unspoken strength of selflessly active love, while the "busy ado" of the others continues and at once covers up the miracle as something quite commonplace: "I saw nothing extraordinary in it any more."[15] And yet in another way it is a moment of heightened awareness, when—from an extreme distance—the inhuman patterns of life and thought, seen through and shattered, prove to be an infernal phantasmagoria of "nothingness" that vanishes when confronted with the "indestructible" element in ourselves. We live in two worlds at once, one schematic and related only to parts of reality, and the other free and encompassing the indestructible whole. Since the schematic world prevails, we never attain to freedom, though we always dwell in it: "He is thirsty and there is nothing between him and the spring but a bush. But he is divided in two, one part of him sees the whole, sees that he stands here and that the spring is right next to him, but another part notices nothing and has, at best, only an inkling of the fact that the first part sees everything. But noticing nothing, he cannot drink."[16] The representation of this twofold world runs through all Kafka's work. This is what makes his work mysterious. If Kafka were to solve the puzzle, to break the silence that covers his whole production like an impervious blanket spread over everything he says and writes, he would betray the truth, exchange it for the commercial lies of the prevalent patterns of thought and words. The greatness of his art lies in the mysterious truth of its images.

Kafka's twofold world is his victory over the schematic single world in which we live today. By unreservedly allowing this single world its rights, he ultimately puts it in the wrong. The labyrinthine contradictions have no issue, are "completely without hope," for they are our human world, and it is "easy" to "prove" that a "disruption of the official organization"—a life of freedom—is impossible, that there is "no room in this world" for it. The miracle is simply not "possible," just as it has long disappeared from our religious forms, which have become degraded to the status of cultural values. There is no way of living in peace with miracles in this world. In this respect the gloom of Kafka's interpretation of the world has a legitimate point in the setting of contemporary history. What else, after all, is meant when our civilization cries out for a "transcendental" world order than a final attempt to rid life once and for all of the miracle? But to allow the existing world its rights in so "despairing" a manner is to put an end to it, for Kafka exposes this world as inhuman, elevates in its face the image of a free life, which is *there*, even if no one "notices" it. "Strictly speaking, one is in despair; still more strictly speaking, one is very happy. . . . How suicidal happiness can be!"[17] says Bürgel in conjuring up the vision of a "disruption of the official organization." The knowledge of freedom, of the truth of the impossible in the midst of the necessity of the merely possible—that is the hatch through which Kafka escapes from the prison of this world and removes the bandage from that part of our nature which notices nothing and hence cannot drink at the spring. Kafka's work, an "end" of our civilization, is the "beginning" of an awareness of "truth" high above and yet within all human forms of living and thinking, which indeed become "human" only by virtue of this truth. In taking away man's every hope of happiness, he makes happiness possible: "Suffering is the positive element in this world, is in fact the only connection between this world and the Positive. It is only here that suffering is suffering. Not in the sense that those who suffer here shall be raised elsewhere because of this suffering, but in the sense that what is called suffering in this world is, unchanged and merely freed of its antithesis, bliss in another world."[18] Absolute suffering, freed of its antithesis, is absolute love: "Who renounces the world, must love all men, for he renounces their world as well. Thus he begins to sense true human nature, which, provided one is its equal, cannot but be loved. To love one's neighbor within this world is no more and no less wrong than to love oneself within the world. That leaves only the question whether the former is possible. The fact that there is nothing other than a spiritual world deprives us of hope and gives us certainty."[19] Kafka's negation of our spirit's civilization is the salvation of the spirit.

As to Kafka the man—who can hope to tell what he was? Our overcontrolled business-oriented civilization has swiftly cast over Kafka, both the man and his work, the convenient net of ready-made thought. It has finished him off with interpretations, dipped him with explanations into the monotonous darkness of cultural diagnoses interchangeable at will, and illuminated his baffling nature sociologically, psychoanalytically, or existentially simply in order to consume him more comfortably. All these interpretations may be right. Kafka himself would probably have made no attempt to refute them, believing as he did that even "one's opponent, the world, must not be cheated of its victory."[20] But the interpretations touch and explain only the periphery of his life, only the conditions in which his work originated, the pains and conflicts that sharpened his vision of the world in which we live, conditions which freed his art from the glittering masks of a literature that seems alive, but is actually wasting away. They do not penetrate the walls surrounding the mind of a man who transformed his own life into a symbol of mankind, always took up a position beyond himself, and created a world raised so high above his interpreters that there can be no contact, let alone any secure steps of understanding, between the interpreted world of Kafka's biography and the world of his poetic creation.

Many attempts have been made to find in the atmosphere and environment in which Kafka grew up an explanation for his extreme spiritual loneliness, for his exceptional position "outside humanity." Franz Kafka was born in Prague, on 3 July 1883, into a German-speaking Jewish family of Czech origin, the son of a merchant. From the first he was never really at home anywhere, was neither wholly German nor wholly Czech nor wholly Jewish, for his upbringing by emancipated, religiously indifferent parents was scarcely influenced by any genuine Jewish religious feeling. But it is characteristic that in his earliest works known to us he saw his own person merely as a random, irrelevant cipher, and he at once developed his own situation in terms of general principles and derived from it an acute analysis of the state of our society as a whole. "Wedding Preparations in the Country," which he wrote in 1907, contains all the elements of his later work. Like a registrar he records everything that floats by in the streets of a big, modern city: "Then a slim lady came into view . . . she seemed unintentionally alien to all passers-by, as though by some law."[21] Already at this stage the alienation of people in modern society is described as a discrepancy between consciousness and an unknown "law" unconsciously lived; the split, in fact, is taken to such

radical lengths that Raban sends his body out on a journey while he himself stays in bed as a beetle. The basis
of Kafka's writing is not the Judaic concept of the law
nor Kierkegaard's theology, but the process of alienation in modern society, a process that he comprehended
very early. Even in this youthful work the alienation is
elaborated in minute detail in the tension between the
"I" vainly trying to enter the anonymous "law" of "one,"
and the "one" never penetrating into "me": "One works
so excessively hard at the office. . . . Yet all this work
gives one no claim to being treated with affection by
all the others, on the contrary, one is alone, quite alien
and merely an object of curiosity. And so long as you say
one instead of *I*, it does not matter and one can tell this
story, but once you admit that it's yourself, it is as if you
were pierced and you are horrified."[22] He did not concern himself with the religious texts of Judaism until
very much later, nor did he read Kierkegaard before
1913 and not intensively until 1917, when he had already written or conceived his major works. "Kierkegaard is a star, but in a quarter all but inaccessible to
me," he wrote to Oskar Baum in 1917.

Similarly, Kafka's alienation from his father and his
home, his studies and his profession, as well as his conflicts in love and his tormented struggle both for and
against marriage originate in a fundamental and deliberate attitude toward life. He disassociated himself from
everybody and everything, and yet acknowledged and
translated into life a strict ethical responsibility for

everybody and everything. During the years when he was at school in a German *Gymnasium* in Prague (1893–1901) and, subsequently, read law at the German University of Prague (1901–1906), he forced himself to "feed the spirit on sawdust, as it were,"[23] while inwardly he already yearned for creative writing. He graduated in 1906, and later took an office job with a Prague workmen's accident insurance company. For eleven years, until 1917, when he fell ill with tuberculosis, he refused to shed the burden of a bureaucratically dry profession, although at the same time he brought to his writing an absolute dedication without parallel: "The vast world that I have in my head. But how to set myself free and set it free without being torn to pieces. And yet a thousand times rather be torn to pieces than keep it back in myself or bury it. That is what I am here for, I am quite clear about that."[24] The same antinomy between disassociation and responsibility underlay the conflict with his father, as is demonstrated by the famous "Letter to My Father" (1919), which, throwing light on the psychoanalytical background, at the same time overcomes it. His conflicts in love, his repeated engagements and disengagements, were the fruit of the ultimate hope and ultimate despair with which he viewed the possibility of love and marriage in a world where life is so arranged that both are always perverted into their opposite. This was clearly stated by Milena Jesenska-Pollak, when Kafka broke off his relationship with her:

What is blamed on Frank's [Kafka's] non-normality is precisely his merit . . . I believe, rather, that all of us, the whole world and all people, are sick and that he alone is healthy, has the right views and the right feelings and is the only pure individual. I know that he does not resist life, he resists only this kind of life. . . . He knows a thousand times more of the world than all the world's people. . . . Always he considers himself to be the one who is guilty and weak. And yet there is no one else in the whole world who has this tremendous strength, this absolute and irrevocable need for perfection, purity and truth. That's how it is. To the very last drop of my blood I know that it is so. Only I cannot quite bring it home to myself. Once that happens, it will be terrible.[25]

When Kafka, after the brief happiness of his life in Berlin with Dora Diamant, died of tuberculosis on 3 June 1924 at the Kierling sanatorium near Vienna, at the age of forty-one, his physician and friend Robert Klopstock wrote: "His face is as rigid, severe, unapproachable, as his spirit was pure and severe—a royal face of the noblest and most ancient lineage."[26] Kafka desired that the writings he left behind should be burned.

4

Franz Kafka between East and West

Franz Kafka stands alone among the writers of our century by virtue of his critical insight into the immanent laws of social and personal reality and his illuminating portrayal of them. This is why he is the most realistic writer of our time. But this is also why he is the most enigmatic and disturbing writer to those who are, more or less unconsciously and uncritically, subject to these laws, or those who identify with them, or those who claim to be agents of their implementation and true helmsmen of history because they understand the laws that govern its course. These helmsmen of our destinies, who believe themselves to be at one with the necessary course of historical development, were and still are bound to regard Kafka's critical exposure of their reality-consciousness as a great and menacing offense to their way of thinking and acting. Reading Kafka must have administered the same inescapable shock to them as to those they despise, who either unsuspectingly, or on account of their allegedly "mistaken consciousness," fall and remain under the sway of the immanent laws of reality. That shock is to find that Franz Kafka exposes the truth of reality. It is so unbearable a truth that they have to lock it out of their consciousness and thrust it into the limbo of all that is forbidden, disreputable, sinister, irrational, or even perverse and decadent.

In the West, the word "Kafkaesque" contributed to this process of repression. It is jargon for everything that the soul unreflectingly cast into nothingness, or the absurd, felt to be nightmarish, impossible to assimilate and master, and heavy with anxiety. In the East such slogans as "irrationalism," "decadence," "extreme individualism," and "terminal phase in the literature of late capitalism writhing in spasms of despair" contributed to a similar but even more radical process of repression, and at the same time provided the justification for refusing to allow Kafka's work to be printed and distributed.

However, as in any process of repression, it proved impossible in the long run to quell the suspicion that Kafka's work represented a possible truth, indeed *the* repressed truth, of reality. When Kafka died in 1924 at the age of forty-one, he was known only to a handful of friends. Today [1963], on the eightieth anniversary of his birth on 3 July, he is an author of world renown in the West, and although we still probe the mystery or misinterpret his work, we do recognize it as unsurpassed in exactitude and artistic maturity. We see him as giving creative form to insights that strike and stir every one of us, whether we turn away from them in horror or accept them. And in the East, at a congress in Prague on this eightieth anniversary, for the first time the serious and exciting question was raised as to whether his work was not perhaps, after all, an expression of "critical realism." As such, it could be taken seriously by those who know and direct the historical laws of man's evolution, if only they think through to the end their own talk of the "dialectical" structure of human reality.

In all Kafka's work two levels of consciousness are seen to be in conflict. The first is the level of pseudo-realistic consciousness, where consciousness clings tightly to the given realities, explains and justifies them, and judges on the basis of tangible, visible, or calculable facts. Here the world can be justified, and morality is unimpeachable because it is guided by the given facts. This pseudo-realistic level of consciousness, which completely dominates our age, was characterized as follows by Kafka:

> Once upon a time there was a community of villains, that is, they were not villains but ordinary people. They always stuck up for each other. If, for example, one of them had caused unhappiness to someone, a stranger not belonging to their group, in a somewhat villainous manner—and that again does not mean villainous, but as is ordinary and customary—and he then confessed to the community, they investigated the matter, passed judgment, imposed penance, forgave and so on. It was not ill

meant, the interests of the individual and the community were strictly safeguarded, and the penitent was handed the complement to the primary color he had shown. "What is the matter? Why do you worry? You did the natural thing, acted as you had to. Anything else would be incomprehensible. You are merely overwrought. Do be sensible again." In this manner they always supported each other, even after death they did not disperse but danced their way up to heaven together. They flew along, a vision of the purest childish innocence. But since at the gates of heaven everything is broken up into its elements, they plunged into the depths, like rocks.[1]

The second is the level of critical consciousness, where the apparent connection between facts and motivations is broken up into its elements and the naked truth appears. This truth, to be sure, is bound to seem monstrous, indeed unimaginable, to the pseudo-realistic consciousness. But there can be no help, no change, unless this truth is thoroughly understood. In his sketch "In the Gallery," Kafka illustrated this by the image of an equestrian whose life is at the same time a true image of the industrial world.

If some decrepit, consumptive equestrian on her unsteady mount were driven round and round the circus ring by a merciless, whip-cracking ringmaster, for months on end without ever a pause, performing before an insatiable public, pirouetting on her horse, blowing kisses, swaying to and fro, and if, to the unintermitted roar of the orchestra and the ventilators, this spectacle went on and on into the indistinct, endlessly extending future, to the accompaniment of the ebb and flow of applause by hands which really are steam hammers—if this happened, maybe some young visitor in the gallery would race down the long stairs through all the tiers, would burst into the ring and shout "Stop!" through the fanfares of the ever-obliging band.[2]

If only, therefore, we were to take a critical look at the reality of our life and recognize how monstrous it is, salvation and change would be possible. But since we do not, since the prevalent pseudo-realistic consciousness regards truth as something fantastic and indeed incredible and the outer façade as truth, there is a hindrance to salvation in this uncritical age of ours. Hence the second part of Kafka's "In the Gallery" reads as follows:

But since this is not so; since a beautiful lady, all white and red, floats in between the curtains raised for her by proudly liveried ushers; since the ringmaster, trying to catch her eye in utter devotion, crouches like an animal in breathless expectation of her coming; lifts her upon the dappled grey as tenderly as if she were his adored granddaughter setting out on a perilous journey; cannot bring himself to give the signal with his whip and then finally, controlling himself, cracks it sharply; runs alongside the horse with his mouth wide open; follows her leaps with a keen eye and can hardly grasp her skill; calls out warning shouts to her in English; furiously demands the utmost attention from the grooms who hold up the hoops; before the great *salto mortale* raises his arms imploringly toward the band to silence it; finally lifts the girl down from the trembling horse, kisses her on both cheeks and thinks the public's ovation is never enough; while she herself, leaning on him, raised high on the tip of her toes, in a whirl of dust, arms outstretched and head thrown back, wants to share her happiness with the whole circus—since this is so, the gallery visitor rests his face on the balustrade and, foundering in the final march as in a deep dream, weeps without knowing it.

This seeming impotence on the part of the critical visitor in the gallery, whose every rescue attempt is cut short by the stolid, self-deceiving reality-consciousness of all the others, turns into an active struggle in other works of Kafka's. This happens whenever critical consciousness, unlike the young gallery visitor, withstands being overwhelmed by the pseudo-realism of its environment, withstands foundering in a deep dream, and has the courage to break through the façade of lies erected by those who today guide the world's destinies and are such past masters at taking refuge in self-justification. When critical consciousness exposes the true content of their thinking and acting, it thereby imparts understanding and resistance also to those who allowed themselves to be walled in behind this façade of lies.

What does this "struggle" in Kafka look like? How does he succeed in breaking through the façade and bringing the truth into consciousness?

It will have been noted that in the first description of the circus rider Kafka really constructed a model of the modern industrial world, in the sense that this seemingly fantastic, unreal act illustrates precisely the essential, predominating principle of the industrial world. The nonstop dynamics of an economy and industry that must ceaselessly produce in order to keep alive are rendered in the image of the equestrian careering around for months on end before an insatiable public, on again into an indistinct, endlessly extending future, to the accompaniment of applause by hands that really are steam hammers.

In his first novel, *America*, which he wrote between 1911 and 1914, Kafka worked out this model both inten-

sively and extensively on the pattern of American industrial society. We may recall how Karl Rossmann, the
hero of the novel, sees in his uncle's telephone room "in
the glare of electric light an employee, indifferent to any
noise made by the doors, his head harnessed in a steel
band that pressed the earpieces to his ears . . . and
only his fingers that held the pencil twitched with inhuman regularity and speed." Questions of his own or
objections against the messages of the partner at the
other end of the line are both senseless and redundant,
for

> certain words that he heard forced him, before he could act on
> his intention, to look down and write. Nor did he have to talk
> . . . for the same messages that this man took down, were simul-
> taneously taken down by two other employees and subseqently
> compared, so as to exclude errors as far as possible. . . . Right
> through the center of the room there was a steady traffic of
> people dashing to and fro on their errands. No one greeted any-
> one else, greeting had been abolished, each followed in the foot-
> steps of the one in front and looked down at the floor, on which
> he wanted to advance as fast as possible.[3]

Everyone runs along the tracks laid down for him,
merely gazes fixedly at the floor on which he happens
to be walking and wants to "advance as fast as possible"
in his career. Everyone is replaceable by everyone else.
In the Occidental Hotel the clerks dish out information
"without a moment's interruption." "Mere talking would
not have been enough for their task; they gabbled,"[4] for
"one knows . . . more or less all the questions that crop
up, and the rest one needn't answer."[5] By a "barely per-

ceptible shake of the head" the unanswered question is tossed back to the questioner, who is thus forced to "formulate the question better,"[6] that is, to make it fit into the pattern.

The crucial point is that in this first novel, which is written in the traditional, realistic form, Kafka, notwithstanding his trenchant criticism, deals only with the universally known superficial symptoms of the principle intrinsic to modern industry. That is why his hero, Karl Rossmann, is just as helpless vis-à-vis this world as is the young gallery-goer. Only in his later novels, *The Trial* and *The Castle,* did Kafka go further and represent the innermost structures of modern consciousness and its associated reality. Only in these works, therefore, and more especially in *The Castle,* does the hero K. engage in an active, critical struggle.

Whereas Karl Rossmann is banished to America by his parents, K. in *The Castle* has by his own decision left his family and his safe professional career in order to take up the struggle against the castle authorities, who, on the one hand, have called him in as a surveyor, and, on the other hand, refuse to let him know anything at all about what he is to do as a surveyor or even about his right to exist within the domain of the castle and the village belonging to it. It is said of the castle and the village: "No one comes, it is as though the world had forgotten us."[7] With this statement Kafka definitely left the world of pseudo-realistic consciousness. The castle and the village represent mankind's reality, which mankind never raises into consciousness. Hence, they are forgotten by the world. It is K.'s wish and duty to survey this forgotten reality. What does it look like?

The castle authorities ceaselessly register and record in endless files, moving along innumerable official channels, absolutely everything that people on this earth think and do. The villagers' lives consist of uninterrupted confrontations with the castle authorities, and they know it. This awareness of necessity makes them appear strange to the rest of the world. The same awareness confers upon them the special position of being the only parish to live in constant contact with the all-knowing and all-recording castle authorities. Since every single fact of our human existence can be interpreted and explained in wholly different and contradictory ways from the most varied points of view, the castle authorities' files forever move from office to office, from one clearance to another, without it ever being possible or permitted to take a final decision. For each human deed or misdeed can be justified, elucidated, explained in terms of certain conditions, which themselves rest upon the inner necessity and logic of life's realities. Or, as the mayor says to K.: "Mistakes do not happen, and even if a mistake should happen for once, as in your case, who is there that can say definitely that it is a mistake?"[8] That is the conclusion of modern thought, which can explain and excuse all human actions on the basis of psychological, sociological, historical, or other general preconditions.

The result is the villagers' complete uncertainty in the fact of the pronouncements, always ambiguous, never final and decisive, of the castle authorities. The villagers know themselves to be the defeated victims of a reality that is utterly incomprehensible to them and yet compulsively associated with them. Their faces give the impression that they have been "maltreated," "beaten flat," and they look as though they lack any will power. They have knowledge, it is true, but their knowledge is guided exclusively by recordable (and that means general and scientifically verifiable) statements about mankind. These statements are as mutiple and contradictory as are the infinitely variable theses of our ambiguous reality in the East and the West.

This is the situation into which the stranger, K., steps, ready for combat. He does not want to lead a "worker's existence" in the village, to become indistinguishable from all the others. He refuses to be interrogated by the village secretary of Klamm, the castle official assigned to him. He does not wish to be registered and controlled. He wants to remain "always free" in his struggle. For this reason he wants to meet face to face not Klamm the official, but Klamm the "private person." This refractoriness of K.'s arouses misgivings. No one wants to shelter him. When the landlady of the Bridge Court Inn throws him out, because he, the "blindworm K.," as she calls him, wants to push his way personally into the presence of the "eagle,"—to her the "high, exceedingly high official Klamm," K. asks her: "You aren't by any chance afraid for Klamm?"[9] On the other hand, by virtue of their awareness, the same villagers have enormous respect for K. They look to him for their "liberation," regard him as their clandestine hero who, like a fairy tale prince, at first sight insignificant and knowing nothing of their world, may one day break their bondage.

Just because he does not know the endless official channels, because he asks and looks and searches for his way as a surveyor in this world governed by the castle, he is indeed, as the Bridge Court Inn landlady says, "in regard to local conditions a terribly ignorant man." But, he replies, "the ignorant dares more."[10] He declares expressly that he wishes to "face a man of power in freedom."[11] And his struggle is defined as follows: "All that the authorities had to do, however well they were organized, was merely to defend remote, invisible things on behalf of remote, invisible masters, whereas K. was fighting for something living and close at hand, for himself."[12] Of the villagers, on the other hand, it is said that they "took for granted" the castle officials and their servants like "a familiar natural occurrence, and only tried to ward off unduly heavy blows; seeking support in numbers they yielded to the current if they had to, and bowed their heads when it became necessary to protect themselves against the hissing breath of the men in their ever unsatisfied search."[13]

Thus in this vast, worldwide official organization, K. alone possesses an autonomous awareness of himself. He alone is a person. Only for this reason can he fight.

And solely by virtue of his autonomy as a person, he succeeds in doing something enormous, something unimaginable, namely, he holds his own within this world reality, even gaining control and domination over it: "He was by this time an adept at playing on this official apparatus, this subtle instrument always intent on some sort of compromise. On the whole, the trick consisted in doing nothing, in letting the apparatus work on its own and in merely forcing it to work by standing there, irremovable in one's earthly weight."[14] Thanks to his self-awareness, K. refuses to allow his personality to be split up and dissolved into general, collective principles, and in return he gains insight into these principles and superiority over them. The officials cannot bear the sight of this K., who stands before them, irremovable in his earthly weight as a person; they shout for help, and fear that the whole organization may be disrupted by him.

The point to note here is that these all-knowing and all-recording officials themselves have no more ardent wish and aspiration than to become persons in their turn, private individuals like K. For the vast, endless paper confusion of contradictory opinions, in which they are trapped, can acquire form, clarity, and the highest moral standards in life and action only in confrontation with a free, autonomous consciousness. It is true that, as the official Bürgel explains, such consciousness would "virtually disrupt the official organization," but it would also mean a quite "inconceivable promotion,"[15] for it would confer upon any given official full responsibility

74

and powers in all matters, big and small. For, in Bürgel's words, "Is not the very smallest responsibility the whole of it?"[16] And such free and personal responsibility for the smallest as well as largest matters seems unimaginable happiness to Bürgel.

The happiness of free, autonomous responsibility is always obstructed in contemporary society for the following reasons:

The all-knowing and all-recording officials, a magnificent poetic image for the structure of modern humanity's consciousness, are themselves unremittingly ruled and dominated by instinctive powers they can neither fathom nor raise into consciousness. They are ruled as well by abstract, invisible, commanding forces and values they likewise cannot recognize and understand, and whose power as idols or taboos they cannot overturn. Like a pack of wild animals, the officials' servants assault the women and girls of the villagers. And these servants, we are told, are the true masters in the castle. They, the unconscious instincts, largely rule the officials' decisions. On the opposite side, the taboos of behavioral norms and moral concepts are ultimately merely the instincts' distorted, inverted mirror image, similarly neither comprehended nor personalized, but reigning over them as abstract commands. Thus instinct and morality forever merge into each other, forever change parts in so inextricable a manner as to defy any genuine moral clarification. Kafka drew an incisive picture of this situation especially in the famous incident of Amalia and the official Sortini, who, a man of the strictest morals living a most retired life, nonetheless makes immoral demands upon Amalia. Because Amalia, alone among all the women in the village, resists these demands and, just like K., refuses to submit to official interrogations and proceedings, she is deprived of every means of existence. Not explicitly, but tacitly, soundlessly as it were, and as though by her own doing, she is excluded from the village community. For she is the only one in the village who *sees* and thereby breaks out of the unconscious power mechanism of modern society: "But Amalia not merely bore her afflictions, she had the brains to understand them, we merely saw the consequences, she saw to the bottom of it all. . . . Face to face with truth she took her stand and lived, and bore this life then as now."[17]

The essential point is that Kafka did not fall into the trap of the false, unrealistic bias common to writers in the West and East. He does not play off the solitary, free individual against society, nor society against the individual. What he shows is that Amalia, by looking into the depths of truth, disengages herself from the village's level of consciousness, which can always see merely the consequences. Thereby she breaks the social spell that binds all the villagers and can no longer vegetate and live like the others. Yet she lives in the village after her own fashion. And the village people—this is the crucial point—respect her decision; they even sense, albeit dimly, that only such insight into the "depths" of truth can lead to the creation of a genuine society worthy of human beings.

K.'s aim is the same. He does not want to stand outside society, a Utopian rebel, nor does he want to surrender to the barbaric principles and practices of society, uncomprehended and masked by lies and ideologies as they are. He wants a society of free persons who have gained self-awareness, who, in their struggle for independence can at the same time "survey the land" on which all the others can live and work in equal freedom, in full responsibility for themselves and the community. Kafka's critical realism, therefore, is at the same time a critically realistic humanism.

The classical heritage of German humanism, which Kafka held in high respect and affection all his life, was translated by him into terms of modern consciousness and poetically recreated without the use of epigonous humanistic phrases. His work belies the caricature that has been made of him. He was neither a desperate, lonely, antisocial psychopath, nor an existentialist dwelling in the "absurd," cast into "nothingness." This caricature, in fact, serves only to depict the state of consciousness of those who made it.

In 1920 Kafka wrote in his diary: "I never felt the pressure of any responsibility other than that imposed upon me by the existence, the look, the judgment of other people."[18] And in his confessions of the same year, under the title "He," we read:

He does not live for the sake of his personal life, does not think for the sake of his personal thoughts. He feels as though he lived and thought under the constraint of a family for which, though it is abundantly rich in vital and mental strength, some law unknown to him yet made him a formal necessity. Because of this unknown family and these unknown laws he cannot be exempted.[19]

It is to this human family, which despite its enormous vitality and mental strength knows neither itself nor its own laws, that Kafka felt obligated in his work. His creative purpose was to acquaint them with themselves and their law.

Literary creation cannot change the world. That is the business of politics. But literary creation can change consciousness. And woe to mankind if the politicians fail to join in this alteration of consciousness. Then the result is that state of affairs Kafka described as follows in one of his sketches:

It was a political meeting. It is strange that most meetings take place where the stables are, by the banks of the river against the roar of which the human voice can hardly be heard. Although I sat on the parapet of the embankment quite close to the orators—they were speaking from a bare, square stone pedestal—I understood but little. True, I knew in advance what it was all about, and everybody knew it. And they were all unanimous, I never saw such complete unanimity, I too fully shared their opinion, the matter was all too clear, talked over so often and still as clear as on the first day; both, the unanimity and the clarity, were oppressive, the mind was blocked by sheer unanimity and clarity, one would occasionally have liked to hear just the river and nothing else.[20]

5

Schiller and the
Antinomies
of Human Society

At the Schiller celebrations in 1859 the whole nation
was at one in paying the poet a unique tribute that
far outshone even the posthumous fame of his friend
Goethe. But an examination of literary developments
since then shows that Schiller's writing and thought
have suffered a progressive devaluation. The critical
attack has been directed at the very heart and substance
of his poetry. Roughly speaking, the contention is that
what Schiller wrote was not poetry, but rhetoric. He is
held to have known nothing of the hidden side of poetry, of the element of the unspoken, the unbidden, in
poetic expression. He is considered to lack the lyric
charm of Goethe's poetry, the mysterious depth of
Goethe's characters. His work is said to be all intent and
purpose, loud grandiloquence, obvious and deliberate

intellectual manipulation, and planned construction. The emotionalism of his language is felt to be unconvincing, his characters to be unnatural, mere fantasies of the mind, exaggeratedly idealistic or satanic, and his images and similes artificial and unorganic. And even his supreme mastery of dramatic technique and stage effects is said to have overreached itself in the invention of the most improbable plots and elaborate complications.

Intimately related to all this is the criticism of the spiritual content of his poetry, of what is known as Schiller's "idealism." Just as Schiller's language sacrificed everything individual to the universal and transformed the voice of the personal soul into a didactic general maxim, so, it is felt, did his idealism preclude any genuine tragic conflict without issue, since it sheltered the catastrophes of his heroes under a saving heaven of transcendental ideas, destroyed the tragedy of individual human life which a dramatist like, say, Heinrich von Kleist carried through to its utmost limit and inevitable end. Thus Schiller was, in the last resort, not a tragic poet. He had never penetrated to the very depths of the "concrete situation of human existence," either in suffering or in expression. His poetry was made of human ideas instead of human life. Hence it is not surprising that, with the ascendancy of vitalism and later of existentialism in the present century, Schiller's star has sunk more and more; in his place Goethe, seemingly closer to life and nature, or Kleist and Hölderlin, interpreted in existentialist terms, increasingly came to the fore and indeed were often played off against Schiller.

At the same time there has been no lack of attempts at rescue operations. Efforts have been made to demonstrate a so-called realistically tragic turn in Schiller's later period, in *Wallenstein* and above all in the *Demetrius* fragment, which relates him to Kleist; but clearly this argument completely misses the point about Schiller's own individual approach and, in reality, discredits it.

The fundamental cause of all these misconceptions and futile rescue operations is to be found not in Schiller, but in ourselves—that is to say, in the conceptions and lines of thought that have evolved during the past century or so and have come to determine our present-day consciousness and feeling. Let us set aside our prejudices and ask ourselves whether we, for our own part, measure up to the greatness of Schiller's thought and poetry; such self-criticism will suddenly reveal Schiller not only as a classical poet "who pleased the greatest masters of his time," but as one belonging to "all times" —and more especially to our own time with its spiritual, moral, and political crises, for which Schiller has a store of answers and interpretations pointing far beyond anything now usually proffered by the exalters of ineluctable tragedy or masochistic doomsday attitudes.

It is true that Schiller is the poet of the universal, and not, like Goethe, of man as an individual developing organically into typical forms in accordance with his own inner law. But for Schiller it is the universal that is our destiny; it is society, the state, history, our reality itself. To withstand it, know it, master it, and translate it into a reality of humane living was Schiller's most pressing concern in all his works, from the social criticism of his early dramas through his great historical works to the late history plays, *Wallenstein, Mary Stuart, The Maid of Orleans, William Tell,* and the *Demetrius* fragment. At stake are the great themes of mankind, not merely the tragedies of individual life:

> For only some grand theme will have the force
> To stir the deeper reaches of mankind.
> Man's thought is shrunken by a narrow round,
> But as his aims are greater, so he grows.
> Now to its solemn end the century draws,
> When poetry finds matter in the real,
> When we behold the clash of mighty souls
> Over a worthy goal, when struggles rage
> For what is greatest among human themes,
> Freedom and domination. And now art
> Upon its shadow stage may set itself
> To reach for higher flights—indeed it must,
> Or else be put to shame by life's own stage.[1]

Art, then, is to be measured against reality itself; it has to prove itself in the face of the conflicts of its time. But historical reality is seen in a perspective entirely different from that to which we are now accustomed. The aim is not, as in the great masterpieces of historism, to describe the separate forces and personalities of history, to define their own evolution and, as it were, explain them from within, nor to understand each epoch and phenomenon as a unique, individual event. In terms of his naive-sentimental syzygy, Schiller would have considered such an objective, fact-oriented view of history as naive thinking, as a naive surrender to facts that deprives the observer of any point of view of his own and leads to the relativization of historical reality, to a neutral acceptance of man's historical deeds and misdeeds without reference to their value, and thus to the neglect and ultimate abolition of every absolute human value, of every moral judgment in the course of history. For to understand everything is to forgive everything.

However, Schiller was not a critical moralist in the narrow sense in which Nietzsche defined and attacked him. Unlike the pragmatic historians of the eighteenth century and present-day public opinion, he did not evaluate history from a one-sided moralizing or ideological standpoint, which in its turn is historically conditioned. Rather was he concerned with the fundamental "critical" definition of the a priori conditions of human history and reality themselves. He wanted to bring to light the a priori contradictions that are necessary constituents of human existence and the reconciliation of which is the origin both of the course and the unity of human life and history. Schiller's purpose in his philosophical writings was to gain insight into the general, antinomic unity of human and historical reality common to all epochs.

What, actually, is man? What, actually, is historical

reality? How can man achieve his own integration? How is historical reality to be shaped to make possible a life worthy of man? These are the crucial questions in Schiller's work. In the passage quoted above from the prologue to *Wallenstein,* he says that the struggle for domination and freedom is the great theme of poetry; this struggle, which he treated in all his plays, is likewise concerned with the fundamental "critical" problem of what are the human conditions that necessarily lead to forms of domination and demands for freedom, and what the anthropological and social conditions by which these conflicts may again and again be overcome and reconciled.

In his *On the Aesthetic Education of Man* (in a series of letters) Schiller analyzed these basic conditions as follows: Man, being possessed of the power to know, to investigate, to control nature, carries within himself the conditions for attaining the highest degree of freedom and self-determination, and also for falling prey to the basest slavery and self-disintegration. For the more man advances in the direction of understanding—knowing and freely creating his world—the more does this world of his become multifarious, fragmented, manifold, and the more does he become dependent upon his own creation and lose his unity and freedom.

This antagonism of forces is the great instrument of civilization. . . . Civilization, far from setting us free, merely creates a new need with every force it develops in us. . . . The inner bond of human nature was broken and the harmony of its forces disrupted by a pernicious conflict as soon as, on the one hand, a sharper distinction among the sciences was made necessary by wider experience and more precise thinking, and on the other a stricter separation of the estates and trades by the more intricate mechanism of states. [Individual, independent life] now gave way to an ingenious clockwork where a mechanical, collective life is generated by the assemblage of innumerable, but lifeless parts. State and Church were torn asunder, so too the law and morality; pleasure was divorced from work, means from ends, effort from reward. Bound eternally to a single, minute fragment of the whole, man himself became a mere fragment; with nothing in his ears but the eternal monotonous rumbling of the wheel he trod, man never developed his natural harmony, and instead of minting the likeness of humanity in himself, he turned into a mere cast of his trade or science. But even the scant, fragmentary association by which the separate units are still linked to the whole does not depend on forms of their own choice and making, but is rigorously prescribed for them by a schedule in which their free judgment is confined. The dead letter replaces the living intelligence, and a practiced memory is a safer guide than genius and sensibility. . . . Thus, gradually, individual concrete life is exterminated to provide a scant subsistence for the abstract whole, and the state remains forever alien to its citizens, because their heart finds no way to it. The governing fraction, obliged as it is to make the variety of citizens more manageable by classification, and to deal with people only at one remove through their representatives, at last loses sight of them completely by confounding them with a mere intellectual construction. In their turn, the subjects can feel nothing but indifference for laws which take so little account of them.[2]

This description might well have been written today. It is an inimitably striking anticipation of the whole problem of modern technology, division of labor, bureaucracy, and the machinery of government. For this problem is an inevitable consequence of man's own nature and of the necessities of life. "The compulsion of needs" and man's attempts to master these needs through wider knowledge lead to the situation described, to that "antagonism of forces," in every civilization, even though it is true that in the twentieth century the antagonism has been intensified to a degree unimaginable in the past. Thus, according to Schiller, the forms of state and society, ancient and modern alike, stem from man's physical necessities, from the attempt to ensure his survival amid external nature. For this reason, Schiller gave the collective name of "natural state" or "need-conditioned state" to all these historical forms of state and society. "But man, as a moral being, could not and cannot be satisfied with the need-conditioned state which is the result of man's place in nature and devised for that alone—and woe to him if he could!"[3] Man as a moral being demands a higher form of state and society, one in which he can freely and completely develop the fullness of his powers, and which, as it were, allows the perfect realization of what is essentially human in man's nature. It is true that this higher form of state and society, or, for that matter, this human perfection, this higher "natural condition" of man, does not actually exist anywhere in the real world, but it is an aim and purpose set to man, an idea originating of necessity in man's rational disposition, demanded by his reason. The consciousness of such a higher aim is the source of all mankind's great movements for political and social freedom. "This," said Schiller, with an obvious allusion to the French Revolution, "is the genesis and justification of the attempt of a nation come of age to convert its natural state into a moral one."[4]

At the same time, however, Schiller elaborates on the unavoidable difficulties, the fatal outcome, of all revolutionary liberation movements.

> Whereas physical man is *real*, moral man is merely *problematical*. When reason abolishes the natural state, as it necessarily must if it is to replace it by its own, then it risks physical, real man for the sake of a problematical moral man, it risks the existence of society for the sake of a merely potential (even if morally necessary) ideal of society. It takes from man something he really possesses, and proposes to him instead something he could or should possess. Thus the great difficulty is that the continuity in time of physical society must not for a moment be interrupted while moral society is forming as an idea, that man's existence must not be endangered for the sake of his dignity. When a craftsman has to mend a clock he lets the wheels run down to a stop, but the living clockwork of the state has to be mended while it strikes the hour, and the task is to replace the moving wheel as it revolves.[5]

Here Schiller states with the utmost clarity the contradictions between revolution and concrete society, between idea and reality, indeed the basic tragedy of human history. Schiller has no intention of sacrificing reality to idea, but neither does he mean to betray the idea for the sake of reality. He is neither an idealist nor a realist, but both together. Physical man, pursuing only his needs, instincts, purposes, and immediate advantages, is for Schiller a "savage" who just lets things drift and who uncritically puts up with the existing order of the natural, need-conditioned state and thereby obstructs any kind of "higher humanity." But the man of abstract reason, the idealist who tries to subjugate reality to his ideas, to sacrifice the natural state to the ideal state, is for Schiller a "barbarian" who meddles destructively with nature and society, suppresses them with the tyrannical law of his idea and his moral demands, and thus uses moral man to annihilate natural man. In short, the idea of freedom becomes the source of servitude, and the ideal state a tyranny.

The savage and the barbarian—these are precisely the constantly recurring manifestations of modern civilized man. In state and society the one finds expression in unbridled, irresponsible decadence and in the exploitations of *laissez-faire, laissez-aller,* and the other in the rigid, revolutionary suppression of the individual and of actual society.

Both alternatives, the physical urge to live and the pursuit of the ideal, are intrinsic to man, who is at once nature and spirit. Each excludes the other, yet man is not complete without both. It follows that each must be both negated and affirmed. On the one hand, reason must abolish the historically real, natural, and need-conditioned state, physical society as such; it must take from man what he really is, for the sake of the problematical, ideal ultimate aim. On the other hand, reason must affirm and uphold precisely the existence of physical society, so as not to destroy it, and hence destroy man as well.

To master this paradoxical situation is the essential problem of Schiller's tragedies and thought. It runs through his discussion of the concepts of the naive and the sentimental, of grace and dignity, ancient and modern, and it appears in the problem of guilt in his tragedies, in which moral man enforcing his moral demands sins against natural man and his real physical society, just as, conversely, natural realistic man sins against the ideal. The profundity of this conception of guilt lies in its arising of necessity from man's nature and his historical reality, with the result that in Schiller's late works this guilt took on the characteristics of invincible fate.

Schiller's classicism lies in his mastery of this paradox without sacrificing either idea or reality, without betraying man's freedom and yet without any Utopian transgression of his natural conditions and limits. His classical balance, his model classicism, consists in the maintenance of tragic tension, of the eternal antagonism in man and society, that is to say in an uncompromising critical protest against every fixed, unambiguous position that might threaten and abolish the wholeness of man and his very humanity.

This becomes clear in Schiller's solutions. The problem he set himself was how to mend the living mechanism of the state while it is running, how to replace the moving wheel while it revolves, how to make the idea alter human society without endangering its very existence. According to Schiller, this can be done neither by the natural nor the moral quality of man, but only by a third quality "which is related to both"[6] and mediates between them. If state and society are dominated by ideas and principles, the result is intolerance, party strife, ideological conflict, blindness to the essential nature of one's fellow men and to the actual circumstances of life in its ever changing reality. If state and society are dominated solely by considerations of material ends and utility, by the pursuit of physical, material gain and personal advantage, the result is chaos and brute irresponsibility. Both situations, which in modern life govern public and private affairs alike to an unimaginable extent, are, for Schiller, an expression of extreme inhumanity, of savagery and barbarism. Both can be overcome only by being negated and simultaneously affirmed, each in its respective antithesis. Principles must no longer be seen in isolation to be faced, as it were, as something other than man, as a law, a commandment, a transcendental idea, but must instead become manifest in their antithesis, in the sensual nature of man itself, that is, they must be lived, must find direct expression in man's nature and actions and in his whole attitude, as though they were his second nature. Conversely, man's sensual nature attains its own fullness only in its antithesis, when it is integrated into consciousness and thereby acquires intellectual and spiritual significance. Only that makes humanity possible, enables people to live together, to respect their fellow men's different opinions and indeed their being different, and to understand each other's nature. For when spiritual principles are actually lived, when we really encounter them in an individual and find them expressed in his very nature, they inspire respect, regard, and love, just as man's sensual nature can be understood and loved only when it is a manifest characteristic of his spiritual and intellectual personality. This means that the gulf between moral demands and nature is bridged, and there is hope, too, for the successful transformation of the natural, need-conditioned state into a moral state. The revolutionary's moral demands will continually readjust themselves in the light of the actual nature and potentialities of society, and in turn the irresponsibility of sensual man, who uncritically follows his nature or submits to things as they are, will readjust itself in the light of an idea of humanity which, like a tacit challenge, marks every human encounter and alone makes it possible. This third quality, in which man's moral and sensual qualities interpenetrate each other, is called by Schiller "aesthetic," because the aesthetic form confers on everything sensual a spiritual significance and on everything spiritual a natural appearance.

But it would be a complete misunderstanding of the aesthetic education of man to suppose that Schiller wanted all people to be brought up as artists or even as aesthetes. Rather, what is required is something much deeper and sterner. What is required of moral, spiritual man is ceaseless criticism and self-criticism of his own ideas, lest for lack of the breath of life they become fixed and rigid and thereby vitiate or even imperil the wholeness of man and his society. And what is required of physical man is the transformation of his natural instincts into spiritual, free self-determination, for only then can he enter into the estate of man in the true sense of the word.

Since, in practice, people always have both a natural and a spiritual side, man himself and his society are faced with both requirements simultaneously; that is, natural, sensual man must not be sacrificed to an idea, nor spiritual and moral man to nature. The road to humanity, which was the final aim of all Schiller's exertions, resembles a path along a mountain crest, where every step into a comfortable, unambiguous position has to be paid for by a fall into inhumanity. When freedom seeks to prevail in its pure, exclusive form, it turns into serfdom. When nature is left entirely to itself and rejects every spiritual and moral refinement, it turns into chaos.

Schiller's tragedies are above all demonstrations of such continual inner alternations. They show to what perils a truly humane way of life is exposed, but also show that it is possible. This is true as much of his first work, *Die Räuber*, in which human law and order are destroyed by the rational, coldly calculating Franz Moor no less than by the impulsive Karl Moor, who spontaneously obeys his natural urge for freedom, as of Schiller's last work, the *Demetrius* fragment, in which Demetrius, inspired by faith in his higher destiny and historical mission, is appalled when he suddenly realizes that his birth and nature by no means make him the direct incarnation of this mission, and thereupon tries to force his idea upon his nature. Another example is the narrow path which Fiesco treads between a humane desire for freedom and a personal desire for power—so much so that Schiller wrote several versions of the drama, in which first one aspect and then the other predominated. It will be recalled, too, how in *Mary Stuart* the two opponents, Mary and Elizabeth, are torn by the conflict between instinct and morality, between humanity and the interests of the state. In general, the mature Schiller, from *Wallenstein* on, was more and more at pains to develop the double nature in his main heroes; thus, his idealized Piccolomini is overshadowed by the complex central character of Wallenstein, whereas in the early works the writer's sympathies still clearly lie with Karl Moor, Ferdinand, or Don Carlos and their idealistic passion for freedom, even though he was consistent enough to condemn these heroes to failure in their conflict with the actual order of society. It may be said of Schiller's plays that they are exceedingly elaborate symbols and changing constellations of the ever unchanging conflict within man and his history. Likewise, the language and construction of Schiller's plays can be understood only by accepting them as exemplary, paradigmatic symbols, rather than naively as mere representations of the real world. The seemingly artificial construction of these plays, the improbable web of intrigue in, say, *Fiesco, Love and Intrigue,* or *Don Carlos,* and the confrontation of this web of intrigue with his doomed heroes' ideal passion for freedom and love are precisely the expression, the symbols, of the irreconcilable contrasts that occur every day in our political and social life, of the machinery in which humanity is destroyed, of the purposeful calculations on which freedom and love founder. But Schiller does the reverse as well, lets the machinery come to grief on itself—witness the despair and human desolation which are the lot of his coldly calculating plotters; and thus, in the annihilation of both protagonists, Schiller invokes the quest for a possible reconciliation of the conflict that determines man's nature and history, and in which we are locked just as much as Schiller's contemporaries.

It follows that the emotionalism of Schiller's plays—the seemingly artificial construction and inorganic quality not only of his plots, but also of his language—arises from an unsparing revelation of the truth of our historical reality itself. The poet's aim is to bring into consciousness the universal truth of our social and political reality, a truth unknown because it is concealed and distorted by our individual feelings, experiences, and destinies; in consequence, his language is passionately rhetorical, it elevates to a level of principle every personal particular, and with its very passion summons mankind to liberation—to concrete, real liberation, not a mere dream. Wrote Schiller in his foreword to *The Bride of Messina:*

> The purpose of genuine art is not a mere passing show; it seeks in earnest not just to give man a momentary dream of

freedom, but to set him truly and really free. And for the very reason that genuine art is concerned with something real and objective, it cannot rest content with the semblance of truth; its ideal edifice is built upon truth itself, upon the firm, deep foundations of nature. Thus art is simultaneously both wholly ideal and in the most profound sense real.[7]

Therefore the less today's generation allows itself to be blinded by delusions in coming to terms with the hidden causes of the crisis in contemporary political and social life, and the more resolutely youth cares about the realization of human freedom—not just blaming our cultural crisis on this or that so-called historical factor, nor retreating with lamentations into personal concerns or "existential insecurity"—the more will Schiller's significance again grow in stature. For the antinomies that Schiller dramatized in his plays are those of our own society.

6

The Enigma of
Faust, Part II:
A Tentative Solution

When Goethe had completed the second part of his
Faust, he did a very remarkable thing. He sealed the
manuscript and refused to have it printed. It was to be
published only after his death. In the last letter Goethe
ever wrote, he gave the following reply to his friend
Wilhem von Humboldt's request to be allowed access to
the manuscript:

There is no doubt at all that it would give me infinite pleasure
to dedicate and communicate these very serious jests in my
own lifetime to my dear, most gratefully acknowledged friends,
wherever they may be, and to know their reactions. But the
times are actually so absurd and confused, that I am persuaded
that the honest efforts I have so long brought to bear upon this
strange structure would be ill rewarded and that, washed up
on the shore, it would lie there like a wreck, and would soon be
buried on the beach by the sand of time. Divided counsel for
divided deeds dominates the world.[1]

This last letter of Goethe's ends on a singularly gloomy note: divided counsel for divided deeds dominates the world. Earlier, in *Wilhelm Meister's Lehrjahre,* Goethe had foreseen the social and political upheavals that growing mechanization was to cause in Europe—he spoke of a battle for life or death that would rage in Europe—and now he witnessed the revolutionary unrest generated by the July Revolution of 1830 in France; he sensed that this new, divided world could have no inner contact with his *Faust,* Part II. The second part of *Faust* would be wrecked on the beach, he felt, and the efforts he had brought to bear upon this strange structure would be ill rewarded.

This gloomy foreboding did, in fact, prove true. When the second part of *Faust* was published after Goethe's death, it at first encountered startled disapproval and, indeed, severe censure. The first impression was that in his nonage the poet had lost his creative ability. The old man was playing, people kept saying of this work; he was playing with trifles and remote allegories, with masks devoid of flesh and blood. And the critics of succeeding generations ultimately always insisted on one particular point, namely, that Goethe had withdrawn from social and political reality and had taken refuge in a world of fantasy. Yet the second part was precisely where he should have concerned himself with social and political reality. In Part I, Faust had been taken by Mephisto through the so-called small world of temptations, through Auerbach's Cellar, the witches' kitchen,

Gretchen's world, and the Walpurgis Night; now, in Part II, he appears at the Emperor's Court, in the great world of politics. Here he should have proved himself a man of action. Or so, above all, argued F. T. Vischer, the foremost nineteenth-century critic of *Faust*. From his struggle with Satan and from the great temptations of political life, Faust should have emerged as, say, the great freedom fighter of the modern era, the champion of real political ideals. Since Faust lived in the sixteenth century, said F. T. Vischer, he should, for example, have taken an active part in the Peasants' War, should have fought for the ideals of humanism, of Hutten or Erasmus, should finally have met his death as freedom's martyr and thus prepared the way for the victory of social and political justice. But what happens, instead, in Goethe's *Faust*, Part II? No real political and social question at all is discussed or treated at the Emperor's Court. Instead of seriously coming to grips with political reality, Faust stages a masquerade in which he himself disappears, unrecognizable in the guise of Plutus, the god of wealth; he invents a trifling mummery that, to boot, is incomprehensible to any normal reader. Faust becomes the mere passive, detached spectator at a court entertainment, and takes no inner stand either for or against the political machinations at the Emperor's Court. The same, the argument continues, applies to the second station of Faust's temptations, his encounter with Helena. Faust should here be tempted by the world of beauty and art. But does he inwardly master this world

99

and overcome it? Nothing of the kind. First, there is the endless and, to tell the truth, once more incomprehensible train of antique allegories, masks, and mythological figures that guide Faust through the Classical Walpurgis Night, with Faust taking no position of his own in relation to them. Then, in the Helena Act, properly speaking, everything ultimately dissolves in illusion, and again without any evidence of some inner decision or transformation of Faust through Helena. Only in the fifth act does Faust at last break through to a positive achievement of civilization, by reclaiming land from the sea and by proclaiming his vision of a future free people on free ground. But even this positive, civilizing action is not shown as a hard struggle with reality, but merely stated in more or less noncommittal terms as a vision.

The effects of this view of Vischer's, in one or the other of its varied permutations, have not spent themselves to this day. As recently as 1933, Wilhelm Böhm published a book on *Faust*, under the title *Faust der Nichtfaustische*, in which he set out to prove that Faust really betrays his Faustian character in the second part and no longer possesses any of his original greatness. Even Friedrich Gundolf's great book on Goethe considers the Carnival in Act I, for instance, as one of the weakest points in the whole of Goethe's work, a petty, playful concession to the court of Weimar and to his time.

It is true, of course, that in the meantime some very distinguished authorities have pronounced a positive judgment on the second part of *Faust,* have tried to defend the work against attacks, and to undertsand it in the poet's own spirit. It is equally true that certain scenes of the second part were always readily accessible to the unbiased reader. Cases in point are the great monologue at the beginning, Faust's descent to the mothers, the inflation scene, and certain sections of the Helena Act, such as the Euphorion incident, or the whole of the fifth act. But large parts of the work, including above all the masquerade in Act I, the Classical Walpurgis Night, and also Acts II and IV, appear to be so overcharged with symbolism and allegory that even the most sympathetic and sensitive reader has to grope his way continuously among puzzles. And so the work as a whole has remained sealed with seven seals for the simple, straightforward reader and, to some extent, also for persons of exceptional perception. A survey of *Faust* studies published since 1900 containing no fewer than 512 entries, which appeared in 1939, bore the very apt title *Der Streit um Faust II* [The Argument about Faust II].[2] We have to admit the deplorable fact that dispute and uncertainty still mark the position of the second part of the greatest of German poetic works. One opinion clashes with another, positive appreciations contend with negative judgments. The question, and it is one of urgent concern, is this: Is an approach possible to the inner meaning of this work? Can the enigma of *Faust,* Part II, be solved? Can we, as it were, see the work with Goethe's eyes and thus come to understand from within the poetic mystery of this strange creation?

First, it may be useful to point out a curious fact, to which most people are apt to pay too little attention. We are all in the habit of going straight on from the first to the second part of *Faust*. After Faust's wager with Mephisto, we expect that Faust will have to undergo further temptations at Mephisto's hands, that he will, as Vischer would have it, now withstand and conquer Mephisto's allurements in the great world of politics or in his encounter with Helena. That would have been the natural continuation corresponding to the design of Part I, and one that was tried in Goethe's lifetime, for instance by Hofrat Schöne. Surprisingly, however, we find Goethe foregoing such a continuation, and not by any means for reasons of senile debility, but deliberately and with full intent. Originally he meant to continue the work exactly in this sense desired by all the critics, but in 1825 he struck out all the scenes he had already written—and some of them were magnificent—and deliberately gave the work an entirely new character. According to the original drafts, for instance, Faust's sleep in the alpine meadow at the beginning of Part II was not to be a sleep of "forgetting," in which his sin against Gretchen is, one might say, temporarily wiped out and forgotten; on the contrary, it was to open the door to new temptations. "Spectral choruses of fame and glorious deeds" were, by means of "visible symbols and pleasing songs" to "dazzle him with the delights of fame, glory, power, and domination."[3] Faust, that is to say, was in fact to become a man of active politics. Mephisto was to try to lure him with new temptations. Fame, glory, power, and domination are the outstanding and dangerous seductions of political life, and over them Faust was to win an inner victory. The further action was planned quite consistently. Mephisto joins Faust and gives him an "amusing and exciting description of the Augsburg Diet." At Augsburg, Faust was to "revert to his former abstruse speculations and demands on himself." In a great discussion with the Emperor, he was to press for "higher claims and higher means."[4] He was to make his entry as a world reformer, to proclaim an ideal of government, and try to win the Emperor for it. But the Emperor, the drafts continue, does not understand him, relates everything to worldly, material things and, bored, begins to yawn. At this critical moment Mephisto steps up and, disguised as Faust,

> argues and swaggers and blusters right and left, backward and forward, into the world and out of it, so much so that the Emperor is beside himself with amazement and assures the surrounding gentlemen of his court that this is an extraordinarily learned man, whom he could listen to for days and weeks without tiring of it. . . . He, as Emperor, had to admit never to have found such a wealth of ideas, knowledge of human nature and profound experience combined in any single person, not even in the wisest of his counsellors.[5]

This would, in fact, have meant continuing in the vein of Part I. Exactly as in Part I, Faust was to develop ambitious plans, and exactly as in Part I he was to have been disillusioned by Mephisto and driven to despair when all his ideals were distorted and debased by Mephisto. The conjuration of Helena, too, was originally planned in this sense. Disguised as Faust, Mephisto was to have conjured up the ghosts, among them Helena, while in the background the real Faust watched this perversion of his ideals with horror and lay in a dead faint at the tumultuous ending. "There is a suspicion of trickery [Mephisto as Faust]. Nobody is at ease about the whole thing."[6]

Goethe had already sketched out these scenes in detail. When, for instance, Faust wants to go to Court alone and forbids the devil to deceive the Emperor with cheap illusions, Mephisto answers:

> Go, let thy luck then tested be!
> Prove thy hypocrisy on all such matters,
> Then, lame and tired, do return to me!
> Man only that accepts, which flatters,
> Speak with the Pious of their virtue's pay,
> Speak with Ixion of the cloud's embraces,
> With kings, of rank and rightful sway,
> Of Freedom and Equality, with the races!

And Faust retorts:

> Nor this time am I overawed
> By thy deep wrath, which plans destruction ever,
> The tiger-glance, wherewith thou look'st abroad.
> So hear it now, if thou hast heard it never:
> Mankind has still a delicate ear,
> And pure words will inspire to noble deeds;
> Man feels the exigencies of his sphere,
> And willingly an earnest counsel heeds.
> With this intention I depart from thee,
> But here, triumphant, soon again shall be.

And Mephisto:

> Then go, with all thy splendid gifts, and try it!
> I like to see a fool for other fools concerned:
> Each finds his counsel good enough, nor seeks to buy it,
> But money, when he lacks it, won't be spurned.[7]

In another sketch, for the scene in which Faust develops his ideals at the Court, Mephisto says to the Chancellor:

> Don't bother, Sir, do not protest,
> The words a man may say in ravished żest
> Remain politically harmless.[8]

Clearly, therefore, Goethe originally intended Faust to join issue with the world of politics, as the critics demand. Similarly, the conflict between Faust's idealism and Mephisto's world-wise and realistic skepticism was to have been developed further. Mephisto to Faust:

> To deal with people, let me tell, you need
> No major stratagem. They'll understand you very well,
> If only you make fools of them.

. . . and:

> To keep a thing a secret to yourself,
> You merely have to say it wisely.[9]

Faust himself was to be true to his original, ever unsatisfied character in saying:

> Baseness lies in consolation,
> And despair alone in duty.[10]

The surprising thing is that Goethe deliberately and with full intent deleted all these scenes and sketches he had already written and gave the work an entirely new turn. There is no mistaking what he said, in a letter to Paris on 4 April 1827, about the second part of *Faust* being entirely different from the first as regards both design and execution:

> Cette seconde partie est complètement différente de la première, soit pour le plan, soit pour l'exécution, soit enfin pour le lieu de la scène, qui est placé dans des régions plus élevées. . . . Vous vous convaincrez vous-même, quand vous le lirez, qu'il ne peut en aucune façon se rattacher à la première partie.[11]

Elsewhere we read that what was required was to break free of the troubled conceptual universe of the first part and to ascend to altogether higher regions and more dignified circumstances.[12] For the Faust of Part I was a subjective, passionate, even barbaric individual, always alternating between high-flying ideals and despair; the Faust of Part II was a man more pure, objective, superior, noble, and dignified. In Goethe's own words, he had, indeed, to extinguish the "subjective, more self-conscious and more passionate individual" Faust of Part I, and to "destroy" him by means of the sleep of forgetfulness in the Alps "in order to kindle new life from this apparent death."[13] Faust, the individual, goes under, and in his place rises the supra-individual, timeless, superior, objective type of man. For this reason Goethe did not make Faust enter into a discussion with the Emperor after the cleansing sleep—Mephisto is now left to do that. Instead, Faust, after his sleep, makes his reappearance in a fancy-dress parade, unrecognizably disguised as Plutus. Of Plutus we are told: "There's nothing more for him to strive for, His eyes watch out for what's amiss" (V. 5556 f.). Faust, who strives eternally, has "nothing more to strive for." We seem to be faced with a complete transformation, indeed a reversal of Faust's whole character. This radical transformation of Faust's character has been overlooked in nearly the whole of the Faust literature, yet it is only when we have grasped it that we can really understand Goethe's abrupt change of direction in moving on to Part II. Faust has nothing more to strive for. He is "Plutus," that is to say, inwardly so rich and so perfect within himself that he can do without the subjective passion of ever unsatisfied striving. Like a spirit superior to the world, he takes a bird's-eye view of the whole political bustle at the Court. "His eyes watch out for what's amiss"; he is the one who helps, saves, watches out for mistakes and weaknesses. He has, furthermore, lost all subjectivity, self-consciousness, individuality. He has become a type. His appearance, we are told, is "open" and cannot be described, for the good reason that it is the timeless combination of all human appearances (V. 5562). He is supra-individual, and in a gay mood Goethe talks of his moon face glowing with fresh, all-round health, and no longer showing any sign of anything passionate, characteristic, personal, or instinctive:

> The healthy full-moon face I see,
> The ample mouth, the cheeks that fresher
> Shine out beneath the turban's pressure,

Rich comfort in the robe he's wearing,—
What shall I say of such a bearing?
He seems, as ruler, known to me. (V. 5563 ff.)

No less than twice in the second part, Faust is granted the grace of a sleep of renewal. And yet a third time, in Act II, during the search for Helena, he is advised to lie down and sleep:

For thee were it better to lie here,
Reviving in coolness thy body,
Outwearied with striving,—
The rest that eludes thee,
To taste and be free:
We'll rustle and murmur,
And whisper to thee. (V. 7263 ff.)

Faust—once so restless, impetuous, titanic, and active —now sleeps. He partakes of the organic, healing, recuperative power of sleep. This is how Goethe, in his concern with polarity, with the wholeness of man, compensates the one-sidedness in Faust's original nature and turns him into a universal type. This fact is most often overlooked even today, when references to so-called Faustian man imply the predicament of this one-sidedly active, Faustian man. Goethe himself overcame and compensated this bias in the second part by Faust's passive attitude, organically anchored in nature and sleep. Another important point is that the characterization in the second part is that of a mask. Faust's original character, as such, remains unaltered. In the initial monologue of Part II he speaks of "ever striving for the highest life," and in Act V there is again a strong emphasis on striving, on never being satisfied, for example, in the scene with one of the Gray Sisters, Care. Similarly, at the end of Act I Faust reverts to a passionate attitude toward Helena, which is overcome only in the third act, when he faces her in sovereign detachment as a lover and master who has tamed passion within himself, as symbolized in the taming of Lynkeus. The Plutus mask is, as it were, an ultimate aim that Faust, the man, has not yet achieved but which he assumes as a counter-image, and through this polarity reaches balance at a higher level. The effect of this is not to destroy the unity of *Faust,* but to create it. For this unity does not consist in linear action and identity of characters, but in the law of polarity and intensification, which, among other things, also determines the relationship between the first and the second part.

But it is not only Faust who is altered in this sense; the whole setting, atmosphere, and action are transposed to an objective, more dispassionate, and lighter level, as Goethe says. No longer, as in Part I, is the drama dominated by philosophical and impassioned dialogues, but existence itself unrolls as a play, and a play, to be precise, in which life's so-called "basic phenomena," the eternal fundamental manifestations of existence, are revealed and displayed in masquerades and opera-like revues. Faust–Plutus himself leads the parade in the first act, when fire threatens to break out, and in this sense he is the ruler dominating the world. He no longer discusses political problems with the Emperor, but reveals to our astonished eyes the eternal, ever-recurring fundamental laws of all political and social life. About the magnificently compact and meaningful representation of these basic phenomena there will be more to say in detail later; for the moment the important thing is to clear our perception for what is radically new in Part II.

As existence itself thus unrolls before us in its eternal principles, Mephisto, too, assumes a different function. Goethe carefully discarded all drafts that could be interpreted as temptation of Faust by Mephisto. Faust is no longer tempted by Mephisto—at least not in the first three acts. Even Helena, as we shall see, is no longer a temptation for Faust, but on the contrary represents the highest form of existence, that is, the pure prototype of all that is beautiful, artistic, poetic. She combines in herself everything that Goethe, the poet, himself loved and revered in classical art. Faust is to be led to Helena in a positive sense. Helena is no longer a temptress. For this reason, even in the first act, Faust, in the Plutus mask, is shown as the "poet," "driven" by the genius of poetry in the person of the Boy Charioteer. In some extant variants, Goethe quite openly calls Faust–Plutus a poet, and in the final text Faust speaks of the genius of poetry as his beloved son. Faust, then, is the father of poetry; the name Boy Charioteer may be explained by the simple fact that Goethe often mentioned in conversation how the genius of poetry—or higher demons and good spirits—had once more today happily guided and

directed him. In other words, Faust and the Boy Charioteer here impersonate Goethe's own existence and
awareness as a poet, and all the treasure of poetry to
which man's spirit and love give him access.

But how does Mephisto fare in all this? There is a
remarkable sketch for the Helena interlude, dating from
1800, where Mephisto appears in the Rhine Valley as
Helena's Egyptian maid servant and says to her:

> And the sacred human rights,
> Are the same for slave and master,
> I don't have to take your orders,
> I can snap my fingers at you,
> You don't own me any more.
> I am Christian, have been baptized.[14]

This is odd. Mephisto calls himself a Christian, talks of
human rights that entitle him to refuse obedience to
Helena. In addition, he is an Egyptian woman. What
does this mean? The passage is really quite clear. Mephisto stands for everything that is non-classical, anti-
classical, opposed to Helena's world of classical beauty
and art. Egypt means the world *before* classical antiquity, Christianity the world *after* classical antiquity. And
the modern world means the ideas of the French Revolution, the sacred human rights, which at that time,
around 1800, were of highly topical interest for Goethe.
Thus Mephisto becomes Helena's real counterpart,
whereas Faust is to be led toward her. Accordingly,
Mephisto's character undergoes a complete change.
When, around 1825, Goethe began to reshape the He-

lena interlude and the whole of the second part of *Faust,* a work he completed in the following years, the "modern world" is represented for him no longer by the French Revolution, but by Romanticism, to which at that time he was in critical opposition. Mephisto, therefore, now defends the romantic world of sentiments, the soulful modern attitude of inwardness, against the plastic, objective, architectural beauty of classical antiquity. That is why in the third act Mephisto praises romantic music as against the classical chorus:

> Hark! the music pure and golden . . .
> All your Gods, the medley olden,
> Let depart! their day is past.
> You no more are comprehended;
> We require a higher part:
> By the heart must be expended
> What shall work upon the heart. (V. 9679 ff.)

Mephisto, the cynical mocker of Part I, suddenly praises the inwardness of romanticism, of sentimental education. The appeal to the heart in modern music and sentiments is played off against antiquity. In so doing, Mephisto indeed turns upon the ancient polytheism. As Goethe and his age saw it, Romanticism really meant all post-classical poetry and art, this is, all art from the migration of the nations onward until the present time. This view can be found in Friedrich Schlegel no less than in Hegel's aesthetics. Christianity, with its otherworldly orientation, is supposed to have imparted a profound inwardness and spirituality to art. In the Helena Act, Goethe's concern is to reconcile modern Christian art with classical art in the encounter between Faust and Helena. This is why Mephisto, as the spokesman of modern poetry, has important positive traits. It is true that he persists in the anti-classical world, but in the classical mask of Phorkyas he approaches the Greek world and accepts the invitation of the classical tree nymph, Dryas, to turn his mind no longer to his home, the German North on the Blocksberg, but to revere the greatness and originality of antiquity as exemplified in the grandiose ugliness of the Phorkyads. Thus Mephisto can pay tribute to Helena with genuine feeling:

> Forth from transient vapors comes the lofty sun of this
>   bright day . . .
> Standing now in all thy greatness, and in all thy beauty,
>   here. . . . (V. 8909/8917)

And when Helena disappears, he even advises Faust to hold on to her veil:

> It is no more the Goddess thou hast lost,
> But godlike is it. . . . soar aloft!
> 'Twill bear thee swift from all things mean and low
> To ether high, so long thou canst endure. (V. 9949 ff)

Mephisto has thus undergone a tremendous transformation, no less astonishing than Faust's own. Mephisto, of all people, admonishes Faust to rise above all mean things and to hold on to the divine part of Helena. Even in the second act, in the Classical Walpurgis Night, he shows himself in a similar mood. There Mephisto appears as the prim and prudish modern Christian moralizer against the shameless nudity of antiquity, which

One must with modern thought bemaster,
And in the fashion variously o'erplaster (V. 7088 f.)

As Phorkyas he defends the genius of Romanticism, even the latest romantic sculpture, "the most daring chisel of the newest age," by means of which he is to hold his own as Helena's peer in the temple of classical art, and thus to reconcile the antique and the modern:

With gods and goddesses then may it fall
To us to stand within the temple hall.

And throughout the third act he keeps moralizing, reminding Helena of all her misdeeds and severely castigating her immoral way of life. His role as Faust's tempter, even his wager with Faust, seem completely forgotten. This is most obvious at the climax of Act III, when Faust meets Helena and enjoys and celebrates the "moment":

No Past nor Future shades an hour like this;
But wholly in the Present—[Helena] is our bliss . . .
Being is duty, though a moment held. (V 9381 ff.)

With this enjoyment of the present moment, one would think, Faust has already lost his wager. But what does Mephisto do? Instead of taking advantage of this moment to catch out Faust and finally bind him to himself, he "disturbs" this supreme, spiritual, and sensual moment of love by entering violently with these words:

Spell in lovers' primers sweetly!
Probe and dally, cosset featly,
Test your wanton sport completely!
But there is not time, nor place.

114

Feel ye not the gloomy presage?
Hear ye not the trumpet's message? (V. 9419 ff.)

There is no word of the wager. Why not? Because Goethe's concern has shifted to something different, to the pure, spontaneous deployment of the basic phenomena of beauty, art, nature, history, existence itself. Mephisto, too, must serve his role in this phenomenological primary series of existential elements. He becomes a partial manifestation of these basic phenomena. It is only in the last two acts, especially in the fifth, that the problems of Part I come to the fore again, the problem of the wager and the original characterization of Faust and Mephisto.

So much, then, for clearing our view as to what is radically new, especially in the first three acts of Part II, that is, those most difficult and most incomprehensible to most readers. The next question is how Goethe treats the basic phenomena of existence in these first three acts.

Goethe himself felt these first three acts to have an inner unity. The first one he wrote was the Helena Act, the third, as the climax of the drama; the first two he described as "antecedents"[15] to the Helena Act, that is, necessary prior stages that prepare for Helena's appearance.

Helena was for him the essence of beauty and art, and beyond that also the symbol of man's creative, productive powers, of timeless, classical culture. The question that preoccupied him was this: How can man, amid the upheavals and fatalities of history, find his way once more to a great, creative achievement, to a classically supreme culture? He wants to show all the paths that lead to it, but also all the wrong turnings that lead away from it and prevent great and timeless creation.

The first act shows the path that leads to Helena from without. Helena is conjured up at the Emperor's Court. The problem here is how to arrive at a timeless, creative culture within the framework of human society and politics. The attempt to reach it from without fails. The conjuring up of Helena at the Emperor's Court ends in catastrophe.

The second act shows the path that leads to Helena from within. It is the organic, natural, genetic way. Access to Helena is sought from her own origins. The attempt succeeds.

Let us now retrace both paths. The first act, which represents the path to Helena from without, turns on the following question: What are the conditions and basic phenomena on which human society rests, and how are creative activity, beauty, and art possible in human society? The masquerade, in which Faust appears in the guise of poet and Plutus, shows in the first place the socially fashionable precursors of art.

> Motley fancies blossom may
> For the fashion of the day, (V. 5144 f.)

The problem of "fashion" was one that often preoccupied Goethe in the course of his life. He always saw fashion as an important preliminary to art and gave it much thought. For him, the problem was also in a very profound way connected with the nature of woman, to whom he attributed an educational potential and preparation for the artist. Woman develops in the artist a sense for beautiful forms, a sense of taste, proportions, and propriety, all of which Goethe always considered as important preliminaries to genuine, mature art, though only in social terms, not as inner essentials of art. This is how we should interpret the Garden Girls' words:

We are fair to see and blooming,
Garden-girls, and gay of heart;
For the natural way of woman
Is so near akin to art. (V. 5104 ff.)

In the dispute between the natural and the "fabricated" flowers, furthermore, we find an intimation that the art of fashion merely tends to imitate nature and thereby to render it artificial. But a deeper problem, too, is touched upon here: the fabricated flowers "blossom all the year," that is, contrary to natural blossoms, they are endowed with timeless duration. This first scene of the masquerade concludes with the significant idea that in art everything is to be found simultaneously, "Buds and leaves, and flower and fruit." (V. 5177) Whereas in nature everything proceeds in a time sequence, art has the capacity suddenly to bring together in a unity all the stages of development and thus, indeed, to make the "basic phenomenon" of plants, all the stages of their development, visible in timeless duration: "All the blossom must fade before fruit can ripen, / Blossoms and fruit at once only the Muses give," we find in one of Goethe's poems.[16] For Goethe, finally, the supreme artist is he who does not simply copy nature, but shapes his creations as organically and inevitably as nature, that is, who has learned nature's laws of development.

After this opening scene, in which art and society are confronted in their external relationship, the inner construction of society itself is displayed in concise allegories. The Woodcutters create the conditions of human civilization. They clear the virgin forests, create space, build houses; they represent rough, rugged labor. Next come the Pulcinelli, who take care of communications, "eel-like gliding," followed by the Parasites, who skim the cream off everything. The Drunken Man and the concluding Chorus represent the climax of work: sociable feasting. Then, by way of polarity, poetry intervenes, and poetry, moreover, in its dated fashionable forms, or as we would say today, the "isms" of poetry— the fashions of naturalism, classicism, romanticism, and so on. The last word among the poets is given to the Satirist, because he alone can recognize and scornfully pillory this debilitating social bondage of poetry. After that, the inner construction of society continues. The Graces represent the original forms of exchange, of social relations: giving, receiving, thanking. It is on these three attitudes that the whole of economic life rests, and equally all social intercourse among men. Next, the Fates guide the threads of individual life so as to keep them in order in the skein of human interrelationships. They are followed by the real plagues of professional and social life, the Furies of gossip, defamation, slander, and vindictiveness. The scene comes to a climax with the cortege of the "Goddess of all active forces" (V. 5456), which is meant to illustrate how it is possible at all to develop any genuine, fruitful, creative activity within the framework of society. Every active individual in society is always torn between fear and hope. Fear of defamation and slander, of the envy of others, poisons his actions, while his hope of improvement and his excessive trustfulness equally imperil his activity. Both—fear and hope—are therefore two of mankind's greatest enemies. Only wisdom can master and bind them, so that they can do no damage. But even when done, the work is still in danger: Mephisto, in the mask of Zoilo–Thersites, belittles and decries the successful achievement.

Thus Goethe, as it were, here indicates the external premises, conditions, and limits subject to which human activity proceeds always and in all human societies, whether in the setting of a small village, a town, a professional association, or a government. After this prelude the real theme begins. Genius himself appears, the Boy Charioteer who alone can lead Faust to Helena. Something unexpected, magical, miraculous, something higher enters society:

On it storms, as to assault.
Clear the way! I shudder. (V. 5518 ff.)

119

A sacred shudder overcomes the herald when these "airy specters" are borne through the crowd in their chariot, but without dividing the crowd, because they are bodiless and eternal. This Boy Charioteer who drives the poet Faust–Plutus, is, as was noted before, the genius of poetry itself. He has much in common with Mignon, in *Wilhelm Meister*. Mignon also is the genius of poetry. Like Mignon, the Boy Charioteer is half-boy, half-girl: "One for a maiden might surmise thee" (V. 5548). Like Mignon, too, he has something enigmatic, nocturnal. "Here is the enigma"[17]—these are Philine's first words in introducing Mignon to Wilhelm. And the Boy Charioteer, speaking of himself, bids the Herald: "Make the enigma's gay solution thine!" (V. 5542) Just as Wilhelm adopts Mignon in a scene of stirring solemnity, so Faust speaks, in Biblical language, of the Boy Charioteer as his beloved son. Originally, the Boy Charioteer was called Euphorion, that is, he was identical with Faust's and Helena's son in the third act. Goethe crossed out this name in the manuscript and wrote Boy Charioteer instead, probably for the mere formal reason that it would be asking a bit much of the public to accept in Act I a character who is born only in Act III. But in essence the two characters are identical. They represent the timeless, ever recurring genius of poetry. Euphorion, too, has some of Mignon's traits. As Mignon, in her restless longing for the infinite and eternal, has a tendency to walk over mountains and summits and forever climbs up on trees and roofs, so

Euphorion leaps higher and higher, eventually flies off into the infinite and falls to the ground. And just as Euphorion radiates flaming gold brought up from the depths as a symbol of the spirit's genius, so the Boy Charioteer digs into a mysterious gold chest and scatters the same flaming gold among the crowd, who greedily snap it up, but see in it no more than material wealth and thus get their fingers burned. To only a few does the little flame of genius, of poetic gift, remain and glow on. Thus the Boy Charioteer is not at ease in this confused human society, amid this avid, restless grabbing for external happiness, and departs into solitude, where alone the true genius of poetry can breathe and work.

And now comes the most powerful, the most awesome and most profound scene of the whole masquerade. Faust has the mysterious chest of flaming gold placed on the ground and draws a circle around it to protect it from the greedy grasp of the crowd. But the Emperor, disguised as Pan, the symbol of the whole world, breaks through the circle and stretches out his hand for the treasures in the chest, which include crowns, chains, and rings—the symbols of political power. At that moment he catches fire. The "world's great All" and his entire court are in danger of burning as a result of their hunger for gold, until the poet Faust/Plutus quenches the fire.

This scene has a profound background. In many of his earlier works Goethe had seen the liquid fire of gold as a symbol of the highest powers of life and the spirit, indeed of all that is good, but also of all that is evil in the world. It is from this symbol that he developed the very origin of good and evil. This highest, noblest of metals, he says, can transform itself into anything. In his symbolic fairy tale of 1794, Goethe took gold as the symbol of the mysterious power of the mind and the heart whose correct application can bring about the rebirth of the world and the liberation of creative forces. In the fragmentary sketches for the Walpurgis Night on the Blocksberg, in Part I, Goethe describes a gigantic, infernal Diet, at which the whole world pays tribute to Satan—kings, ministers, writers, men and women alike. The devil seduces them with flaming gold, which appears in two forms: first as greed for money, as Mammon, whose golden glow casts an eery, lurid light upon the whole mountain, and second as desire for sexual love, for earthly immortality through biological procreation. Gold represents man's elementary power of life and love, which in the first instance is neither good nor evil. If man merely wants to possess this power, to degrade it for his own enjoyment alone, it becomes the source of all evil, avarice, and selfish sexuality, the true elements of evil. But if man uses this power serenely and spontaneously, in a selfless striving for the divine, it becomes the source of genius, of all that is beautiful and good, the genuine power of creation. Thus, in the hands of the Boy Charioteer, gold is the real creative power of genius. But in the hands of Mephisto, who in this masquerade appears as a Starveling, a thin old miser wanting to possess everything in contrast to the inwardly rich and generously giving, selfless poet Plutus, gold becomes the symbol of base sexuality. Mephisto as avarice degrades and distorts this supreme power of love and the spirit into baseness and evil. Correspondingly the Emperor, disguised as Pan, with his greed for crowns and chains and rings—that is, for power—unleashes the world catastrophe, the downfall of political and social life.

At the same time, however, the Emperor's contact with the liquid gold, this primordial power of life, had not only a negative, but also a positive significance. It gave him a glimpse of the elementary laws and secret foundations of political life. In the scene that immediately follows the masquerade, the Emperor describes a strange occurrence. When the flames pressed in upon him, he felt as though he were in Pluto's realm, in the underworld. Even there he was a prince and the ruler of the fire.

> Through the far space of spiral shafts of flame
> The long processions of the people came, (V. 5997 f.)

All the peoples paid homage to him. He stood at the center of human history. He, therefore, becomes master over this primordial force of life, this flaming liquid gold; he is not conquered by it, but withstands it and uses it selflessly and correctly. He thereby also overcomes everything negative in political life, and in a very positive way takes his sovereign, serene, and superior place in the whole of the earth's existence. For the text goes on to describe how the Emperor could similarly become master over water, air, and land, ruler of all the four elements, of the whole cosmos, if only he had the courage to face these primordial forces without fear, to leap into them regardless of his own safety:

> Obedient Fire is tested now by thee;
> Where wildest heaving, leap into the Sea.
> . . . There gorgeous dragons, golden-armoured, float;
> There gapes the shark, thou laughest in his throat.
> (V. 6005 ff.)

Death and rebirth, ruin and renewal of earthly existence —life's extremes are here put before us by Goethe in magnificent and striking symbolism.

Goethe, therefore, did not evade taking issue with the so-called great world, but instead projected it onto an infinitely more profound, timeless plane. He explores the source and origin of all evil, of catastrophes and war. Say the Gnomes:

> Yet we the stores of gold unseal,
> That men may pander, pimp and steal;
> Nor iron shall fail his haughty hand
> Who universal murder planned:
> And who these three Commandments breaks
> But little heed o' the others takes.
> For that we're not responsible:
> We're patient—be you, too, as well! (V. 5856 ff.)

Goethe is here seeking to apprehend symbolically the essential, eternal causes of war.

All this becomes even clearer in the following scene.

Mephisto gives the Emperor not genuine gold, but paper money in lieu of the treasure of gold in the earth. It is a description of a modern inflation, a huge economic fraud. The genuine is replaced by an illusion. This, for Goethe, was the real trouble with modern economic and political life.

Having reduced social and political life to eternal phenomena, Goethe similarly lets Faust conjure up Helena from eternity itself. Faust descends to the Mothers, who dwell outside time and space, where the eternal prototypes of all things, also of Helena, are to be found. What gives him access to the Mothers is a key of flaming gold, once more the element that symbolizes the supreme power of life and the spirit.

But again the desire to possess Helena prevents her being truly won. When Faust passionately wants to embrace Helena, catastrophe ensues. With an explosion, the spirits dissolve in vapor. Faust falls to the ground in a dead faint. Beauty cannot be transplanted from eternity into this world suddenly and without an intermediary, and every attempt to do so is bound to fail. Goethe furthermore illustrates how beauty and art must inevitably be misunderstood in mere social life. Everyone wants to draw art down to himself, instead of rising toward it by strenuous effort. Thus the men want only to possess Helena; the women, the beautiful Paris. No genuine access to art has as yet been found.

After this catastrophe of the first act, there follows Faust's inner, natural path to Helena. Act II is that of genesis, of Helena's birth. In the very first scene Faust, in his study, dreams of Helena's conception and birth. This inescapably implies also the birth of creative genius itself. Goethe here approaches the tremendous problem of the origin of genius. How does genius come into being? How can it become a living, creative force? This is why Goethe causes genius to be generated, produced before our eyes, and Helena's birth to be seen and interpreted; and he does so in the shape of Homunculus, the subject of so much speculation. Homunculus has all the features of the Boy Charioteer and Euphorion. Again, he is half-boy, half-girl, a glowing flame. Goethe himself called him a genius, a creatively active *Daimonion* with a tendency toward the beautiful. But unlike the Boy Charioteer, he does not come to Faust out of the air, as it were, into which he again dissolves. The problem, rather, is this: how can this genius be born, how can he enter into real life and engage in creative activity? This problem governs the whole of Act II. This act begins with the illusory, artificial production of Homunculus in the glass phial and ends with his genuine, organic birth and origin in the waters of the Aegean Sea, as a result of the glass phial being shattered on the chariot of the goddess of love and the spiritual flame being united with the elements of life.

In Faust's northern laboratory, the Boy Charioteer is only half born, only artificially generated. He is merely spiritual, possesses no body. One might say: pure intellect without connection with life. In the drafts he appears as an erudite know-it-all, a historical, world-almanac imp who surveys all of world history from Adam to the present, rattling off the facts of world history during the air trip to Greece until Faust and Mephisto are quite overwhelmed. He is purely artificial spirit devoid of creative, vital force.

> He is, as I myself have heard him say,
> (The thing's a marvel!) only born half-way.
> He has no lack of qualities ideal,
> But far too much of palpable and real.
> Till now the glass alone has given him weight,
> And he would fain be soon incorporate.
> Thou art a genuine virgin's son:
> Finished, e'er thou shouldst be begun! (V. 8247 ff.)

The paradox of the spirit that has existed in all eternity, but must in fact first be generated, if truly perfect artistic creation is to be possible, is here illustrated in magnificent symbolism. Under this aspect, too, Homunculus resembles Mignon, who says: "Let me be apparent until I can be real,"[18] and who in the first place was likewise born in an unnatural way. It was always the same great problem that preoccupied Goethe, the problem of how the spirit, the idea, can assume living, active, and artistic *shape*. The birth of Helena and the birth of this genius are, as Wilhelm Hertz[19] pointed out, one and the same thing. Goethe therefore deliberately deleted Faust's bringing Helena from Hades as redundant, once he had shown the full birth of Homunculus at the end of Act II and once he had brought this act to its conclusion in a triumphal hymn to the god Eros and the four elements fire, water, air, and earth, from which stems all life.

With this the theme of the whole second act has assumed, from within, vast dimensions beyond all measure. Goethe is not really concerned with the historical figure of Helena, but with the creation of being as such, that is, with the representation of the ultimate sources and origins of the cosmos. And in fact the third act does illustrate the genesis of the earth, of life, of the gods, of history and its ever recurring wars, of art, and so on, in a seemingly confusing abundance of mythological figures and events—that is, their symbolic genesis, not, of course, their real one. How can something great, something eternal be forever repeatedly generated on earth—that is the great, overriding question in this most stupendously daring feat of poetry known to mankind.

It is not possible to discuss here all the lines and interpretations of this work, whose composition is really marvellously clear. Only the most important points will be mentioned. The central feature of the Classical Walpurgis Night is the great volcanic earthquake, which symbolizes human revolts, wars, and party strife. Political unrest of this kind is what really disrupts any organic construction and any genuine creative development, and therefore it has to be overcome. This earthquake throws up the mysterious gold, which at once becomes the subject of violent party strife between the Pygmies and the Cranes, that is, the democrats and the aristocrats. In Goethe's early fragment of a novel, "Die Reise der Söhne Megaprazons" [The Travels of Megaprazon's Sons], which he wrote at the time of the French Revolution, pygmies and cranes already symbolize democrats and aristocrats. When writing the Classical Walpurgis Night, Goethe went back to this fragment and in rereading it annotated it in pencil. This party strife can be traced through considerable parts of the Classical Walpurgis Night. It is for Goethe a constantly recurring basic phenomenon in history. It is in the background of the battle of Pharsalus that is conjured up at the beginning, the battle between the dictator Caesar and Pompey, the representative of the old freedom; it is a sort of permanent battle that rages through the Middle Ages between the Guelfs and the Ghibellines and broke out anew in the French Revolution. Even the dispute between the classics and the romantics, which is another feature of the Classical Walpurgis Night, is seen by Goethe as a recurrence of this, for him, ultimately senseless party strife. In Act IV we read:

> At last, the Devils find a hearty
> Advantage in the hate of Party
> Till dread and ruin ond the tale:
> Repulsive sounds of rage and panic,
> With others, piercing and Satanic,
> Resound along the frightened vale! (V. 10777 ff.)

A meteor, suddenly falling from heaven, puts an end to all these party squabbles by destroying friend and foe alike. The meteor always served Goethe as a symbol for a demonic and dreadful event, as in the case of Napoleon. A revolt "from below and above" upsets everything. And yet—and this gives a clear indication of Goethe's own attitude—this whole political and historical upheaval and unrest are only deception and appearance. "Be still! 'Twas but imagined so," says Thales (V. 7946). No genuine creative reality can be attributed to it at all. It is a repulsive, senseless confusion, as indeed for Goethe all historical struggles were more or less lunatic disturbances of the ever identical, organically developing power of nature and the spirit—disturbances resting on fanaticism, dogmatism, and barbarity.

Helena is found by another path. In the midst of all the turmoil, Faust is told to go to sleep by the waters of Peneus. He finds the organic, natural way to Helena, by traversing all the prior stages, all the transformations from the elemental through the human to the divine. But the gold, which gave rise to the dispute, is returned to the sea and thus to its pure, divine origin. During this pageant of the sea at the end of Act II, time stands still: "The Moon delaying in the Zenith," say the stage directions (V. 8034a). History holds her breath. All is ready for the eternal to emerge. During all the millennia of wars raging on the surface, the goddess of love and beauty has eternally guarded in mysterious caves the beautiful and the great. Now it must be won anew. And it is won by the fusion of the divine and the elemental. Ocean nymphs, in whom the divine and the elemental are combined in marvelous purity, go to fetch the gods, the Cabiri from Samothrace, in whom Goethe illustrates step-by-step the genesis of the divine. Then the divine appears in human shape, in the Greek sculptures. But even these "forms of Gods" must be melted down again to make room for eternal transformations and re-creations on earth. At the appearance of the goddess of love and beauty herself, the genius Homunculus smashes his glass. The spiritual is wedded to life. And an endless chain of creative birth and rebirth will begin on earth, sparked off by the ever recurring encounter of the divine and the human. That is the meaning of the second act. Only now can Helena herself appear, the personification of beauty and art. Now the truly great is born.

Act III brings Faust's encounter with Helena. This encounter, too, has a wider meaning. How is a rebirth, a new classicism possible in modern Europe? That is the problem of the third act. Helena is taken into the modern, Christian world, into a Gothic castle. Her encounter with Faust gives birth to modern poetry. Helena discovers the musical, sonorous rhyme, which was absent in ancient poetry. She is introduced to the more profound, more heartfelt depths of Christian poetry. The birth of Euphorion marks also the birth of romantic, operatic music. Greek polytheism is left behind, Nordic tribes take possession of Greece, but not in the sense of military conquest:

Now let our throne become a bower unblighted,
Our bliss become Arcadian and free! (V. 9572 f.)

Politics give way to a higher culture, in which man finds the way back to his pure, natural, god-like origins:

> We wonder; yet the question still remaineth,
> If they are men, when Gods they seem.
> So was Apollo shepherd-like in feature,
> That other shepherds were as fair and fleet;
> For where in such clear orbit moveth Nature,
> All worlds in inter-action meet.
> Thus hath success my fate and thine attended;
> Henceforth behind us let the past be furled!
> O, feel thyself from highest God descended!
> For thou belongest to the primal world. (V. 9556 ff.)

Man is reborn in the knowledge that he is one with the highest god. He stands once more at the pure origin of existence, even in the midst of the present's confusion. Thus this Helena Act, which retraces three thousand years of European development in a symbolic flash, represents the reconciliation of classical and Christian culture. It stands for Goethe's own classicism, in which Christianity and antiquity are fused in miraculous unity. But Goethe knows that this classicism is nothing rigid and unique. It will have to dissolve and give way to a new, creative transformation. This is why the Helena Act leads up to the profound conclusion of disassociating the elements from which this supreme form of classicism has developed. Euphorion's flame of genius ascends to heaven, to eternity, but he leaves behind his garment, that is, the external styles and forms of poetry, which give rise to new literary schools:

The Flame has vanished where it hovered,
Yet for the world no tears I spend.
Enough remains to start the Poets living,
And envy in their guilds to send;
And, if their talents are beyond my giving,
At least the costume I can lend (V. 9956 ff.)

In other words, the costume, the external forms of poetry, will be copied in later years and thus give rise to new schools of art. Helena herself, however, beauty as such, remains in Hades as an immortal personality. Individuality, the name, is preserved. The personality of beauty has become immortal. But the natural elements that were its ingredients are impersonal. They revert to nature. Leader of the Chorus:

Who hath not won a name, and seeks not noble works,
Belongs but to the elements: away then, ye!
My own intense desire is with my Queen to be;
Service and faith secure the individual life (V. 9981 ff.)

The girls' return to nature is symbolized by Goethe by means of their transformation into the elements, into fire, water, air, and earth, those same elements out of which beauty was born at the end of Act II. Now, at the vintage feast, a bacchanalian riot breaks out. Chaos once more prevails.

The cloven hoofs tread down all decent custom;
All the senses whirl bewildered, fearfully the ear is stunned
(V. 10034 f.)

The classical form is smashed. But the Helena drama closes with the hope of rebirth:

For, the fresher must to garner, empty they the ancient skin
  (V. 10038)

Or, at Euphorion's death:

But new songs shall still elate them:
Bow no longer and deplore!
For the soil shall generate them,
As it hath done heretofore. (V. 9935 ff.)

The great circle is completed. The birth and end of a classical culture have been retraced under all conceivable aspects in timeless types and forms, and we are shown the possibility of the birth of a new classical art from the same elements.

And here, by and large, is the answer to the enigma of *Faust,* Part II. The two following acts can be understood in their own terms. They treat the ultimate questions of faith, of the question of man's conquest of death, of the question of redemption. Goethe tried to solve these questions in a universal sense, so universal indeed that it cannot easily, or at all, be reduced to a formula. Christian and humanistic elements are inextricably interwoven. Man's innate ceaseless striving is rewarded, even if it led him through profound guilt and error. This seems to be humanistic, to speak of trust in man's own creative powers, his powers for good. But Goethe also explicitly stresses the limits of these human powers. Man cannot be redeemed by his own effort. He needs grace and love from above. This is Christian. That is why, quite logically, the work ends in Christian symbols and sacred ceremonies. It is not possible here to enter in detail into the strange combination of Catholic, Protestant, and humanistic elements in Goethe. It would demonstrate that in Goethe the Western world reached a synthesis of nearly all the religious, philosophical, and cultural currents, such as can hardly be found in such far-reaching unity and compactness, either before or after him.

And this brings us to the important final question, namely, what is the significance of *Faust,* Part II, for our own age? It will have become clear that Goethe did not evade political questions and catastrophes, but that he sought to define and master them on the basis of fundamental premises. Goethe sought out the very origin of evil, of wars, revolutions, and party strife. Nevertheless, he also took a very realistic view of human society, its economic and other crises. We may recall, for instance, the description of inflation in Act I. And Act V shows us the destructive, murderous power of technology in all its frightfulness, when Faust's civilizing activity on the seashore involves the destruction of godly, pure humanity in the shape of Philemon and Baucis:

Nightly rose the sounds of sorrow,
Human victims there must bleed:
Lines of torches, on the morrow,
Were canals that seaward lead. (V. 11127 ff.)

The whole horror of the technological age is presaged in these lines.

But Goethe considered also the reversal of the dialectical process. Genius is born and becomes creative only when it steps out of itself, when, "moved by the impulse of love," it smashes its artificial glass phial and is prepared unreservedly to sacrifice itself, to give itself up even at the risk of death to the overwhelming powers of existence, the elements—to face them, enter into them. Goethe spelled this out with precision in *Pandora,* where Prometheus, for all his ceaseless activity and for all the strength of his will cannot attain to divinity because he relies far too much upon himself, on his own human powers. Even his more spiritual brother Epimetheus cannot attain to divinity in spite of his spirituality, of his yearning, artistic work, because he is too self-centered. God's blessing is granted only to the children Phileros and Epimeleia, who have the courage to give themselves over unconditionally to death and the elements, to sacrifice themselves:

> From the waves then Phileros advances,
> From the flames comes forth Epimeleia; . . .
> Thus in love united, doubly splendid,
> They embrace the world. And straight from heaven
> Words and deeds come down with many blessings,
> Gifts descend that never have been dreamed of. (V. 1053 ff.)

Note then:

> You below it is who feel what's wanted;
> They above who know what shall be given.
> Titans are you, mighty works you've started;
> But to know eternal goodness, beauty,
> Is a task for gods; let them perform it." (V. 1081 ff.)

All the catastrophes, all evils in the world are caused by man pressing into finite limits the divine spark that burns within him, which Goethe expressed by the symbol of the flaming gold, by man selfishly and greedily wanting to possess it, making it subservient to empirical, purposeful thought. All disaster then stems from Mammon and from the perversion of divine love into mere possessive lust. But evil can again be turned into good, if man serenely and freely sacrifices himself, conscious of the power of love at work within him as the divine flame, the spirit. Then man is promised rebirth, and indeed, like the Emperor after the "jugglery of flame," even genuine, true domination over the elements that earlier threatened to destroy him.

This work of Goethe's also contains a hidden criticism of our own writers and poets. They will never rise to being critical of their age, that is, superior to it, until they try to realize in their consciousness those truths that Goethe expressed in this work. For poetic criticism, caught in its own subject by merely retracing its contradictions, must indeed rightly reject every "way out" as a lie and must remain in a state of despair like the "trapped, passionate individual" Faust: "And despair alone is duty." But poetic criticism can become genuinely "radical" only by pushing its questions and creative forms down to the very "roots," to power, love, and spirit. Only such sovereign awareness can fearlessly retrace the basic phenomena of human reality and thus break out of the infernal circle of our empirical thought and once more transform the searing flame of gold, around which the battle still rages today, into the pure flame of love and spirit. Then our activity will again find the way to new creation, as Goethe presaged around the turn of the century, in January 1800, in "Palaeophron and Neoterpe" (V. 178 ff.)—in words that seem addressed directly to ourselves:

> Men and women, listen to my words of truth.
> What makes people happy is activity,
> Achieving useful things and able to transform
> The evil into good by its divine effect.
> Get up, then, at the break of day, and though you may
> Find yesterday's constructions crumbled overnight
> Set to like busy ants and clear the ruins out.
> Devise your plans anew, employ new ways and means.
> If then the world itself be out of joint and race
> To its destruction of its own accord, you shall
> Rebuild it once again, for everlasting joy.

Notes

The pages given below for quotations from Kafka's works refer to the page numbers of the Franz Kafka, *Gesammelte Werke* [Collected Works], eight volumes, edited by Max Brod, Frankfurt a.M., published by S. Fischer Verlag. Quotations from the writings of Kafka, as well as comments about Kafka, were put into English by the translators of the essay.

Franz Kafka: A Portrait

1. *Gespräche mit Kafka,* p. 88, Gustav Janouch, ed. *Conversations with Kafka,* New York: Frederick Praeger, 1953.
2. *Tagebücher,* p. 21. *The Diaries of Franz Kafka 1910-23,* Max Brod, ed. Harmondsworth: Penguin Books, 1964, and New York: Schocken Books, 1948, 1949.
3. Ibid., p. 545.
4. *Hochzeitsvorbereitungen auf dem Lande und andere Prosa aus dem Nachlass,* p. 121. *Wedding Preparations in the Country,* translated by Ernst Kaiser and Eithne Wilkins, London: Secker and Warburg, 1954.

5. *Das Schloss,* p. 157. *The Castle,* translated by Willa and Edwin Muir, London: Secker and Warburg, 1930, and New York: Alfred A. Knopf, 1930.
6. Ibid., p. 449.
7. Ibid., p. 81.
8. "Beim Bau der chinesischen Mauer," *Beschreibung eines Kampfes,* p. 79 ff. "Building the Great Wall of China," *The Great Wall of China and Other Pieces,* translated by Willa and Edwin Muir, London: Secker and Warburg, 1946, and New York: Schocken Books, 1946.
9. "Die Abweisung," *Beschreibung eines Kampfes,* p. 89 ff. "The Refusal," *Description of a Struggle,* translated by Tania and James Stern; and Willa and Edwin Muir, London: Secker and Warburg, 1960.
10. *Das Schloss,* p. 278 ff. *The Castle,* op. cit.
11. *Der Prozess,* p. 79. *The Trial,* translated by Willa and Edwin Muir, London: Gollancz, 1937, and New York: Alfred A. Knopf, 1937.
12. *Hochzeitsvorbereitungen auf dem Lande und andere Prosa aus dem Nachlass,* p. 98. *Wedding Preparations in the Country,* op. cit.
13. *Das Schloss,* p. 354 ff. *The Castle,* op. cit.
14. "Forschungen eines Hundes," *Beschreibung eines Kampfes,* p. 256. "Investigations of a Dog," *The Great Wall of China and Other Pieces,* op. cit.
15. "Das Ehepaar," *Beschreibung eines Kampfes,* p. 129. "The Married Couple," *The Great Wall of China and Other Pieces,* op. cit.
16. "Er," *Beschreibung eines Kampfes,* p. 299. "He," *The Great Wall of China and Other Pieces,* op. cit.
17. See note 13.
18. *Hochzeitsvorbereitungen auf dem Lande und andere Prosa aus dem Nachlass,* p. 108. *Wedding Preparations in the Country,* op. cit.
19. Ibid., p. 46.
20. Ibid., p. 44.
21. Ibid., p. 33.

22. Ibid., p. 8.
23. "Brief an den Vater," *Hochzeitsvorbereitungen auf dem Lande und andere Prosa aus dem Nachlass,* p. 207. *Letter to My Father,* New York: Schocken Books, 1954.
24. *Tagebücher,* p. 306 (Juni 1913). *The Diaries of Franz Kafka, 1920-23,* op. cit.
25. Max Brod, *Franz Kafka, Eine Biographie. Erinnerungen und Dokumente,* 3rd ed., Frankfurt a.M.: S. Fischer Verlag.
26. Ibid., p. 260.

Franz Kafka between East and West

1. "Eine Gemeinschaft von Schurken," *Hochzeitsvorbereitungen auf dem Lande und andere Prosa aus dem Nachlass,* p. 80 f.
2. "Auf der Galerie," *Erzählungen,* p. 154 f. "Up in the Gallery, *The Penal Colony,* translated by Willa and Edwin Muir, New York: Schocken Books, 1948.
3. *Amerika,* p. 58 f. *America,* translated by Willa and Edwin Muir, London: Routledge, 1938, and Norfolk: New Directions, 1940.
4. Ibid., p. 221.
5. Ibid., p. 224.
6. Ibid., p. 222.
7. *Das Schloss,* p. 421. *The Castle,* op. cit.
8. Ibid., p. 90.
9. Ibid., p. 79.
10. Ibid., p. 78 f.
11. Ibid., p. 71.
12. Ibid., p. 80.
13. Ibid., p. 449.
14. Ibid., p. 433.
15. Ibid., p. 354.
16. Ibid., p. 352.
17. Ibid., p. 278 ff.
18. "Hochzeitsvorbereitungen auf dem Lande," *Hochzeitsvor-*

bereitungen auf dem Lande und andere Prosa aus dem Nachlass, p. 303. "Wedding Preparations in the Country," *Wedding Preparations in the Country,* op. cit.

19. "Er," *Beschreibung eines Kampfes,* p. 295. "He," *The Great Wall of China and Other Pieces,* op. cit.

20. "Hochzeitsvorbereitungen auf dem Lande," *Hochzeitsvorbereitungen auf dem Lande und andere Prosa aus dem Nachlass,* p. 256. "Wedding Preparations in the Country," *Wedding Preparations in the Country,* op. cit.

Schiller and the Antinomies of Human Society

1. *Wallenstein,* Prologue.
2. *Briefe über die aesthetische Erziehung des Menschen. On the Aesthetic Education of Man.* In a Series of Letters. Fifth and sixth letters.
3. Ibid. Third letter.
4. Ibid. Fourth letter.
5. Ibid. Third letter.
6. Ibid. Third letter.
7. *Die Braut von Messina. The Bride of Messina.*

On the Aesthetic Education of Man, translated by Reginald Snell, was published by Routledge & Kegan Paul Ltd., London, 1954, and Frederick Ungar Publishing Co., New York, 1965.

Wallenstein, translated by Charles E. Passage, was published by Frederick Ungar Publishing Co., Inc., New York, 1960.

The Bride of Messina was published in one volume with *William Tell* and *Demetrius,* translated by Charles E. Passage, Frederick Ungar Publishing Co., New York, 1962.

Notes

The Enigma of Faust, Part II

Translations from *Faust* are from the English of Bayard Taylor; all other quotations are translated by the Hendersons.

1. *Gedenkausgabe* [Memorial Edition] Vol. 21, p. 1043.
2. Ada M. Klett, *Der Streit um Faust II seit 1900.* Jenaer Germanistische Forschungen 33. Jena 1939.
3. *Faust II,* Paralipomena 63. Weimarer Ausgabe 15/2, p. 173 f.
4. Ibid. p. 174.
5. S.H.G. Gräf, *Goethe über seine Dichtungen,* II, 2., No. 1188, p. 240 [20 December 1916]; cf. Weimarer Ausgabe I, 15/2, p. 173 ff.
6. *Faust II,* Paralipomena 63, *loc. cit.* p. 175.
7. Paralipomena 68, *loc. cit.* p. 180 f.
8. Paralipomena 69, *loc. cit.* p. 181.
9. Paralipomena 72 and 75, *loc. cit.* p. 181 f.
10. Paralipomena 83, *loc. cit.* p. 183.
11. To Stapfer, 4 April 1827. Printed in Gräff II, 2, No. 1474, p. 389 f.
12. *Faust II,* Paralipomena 123, *loc. cit.* p. 199.
13. *Gespräche IV* [Conversations] IV, p. 329.
14. *Faust II,* Paralipomena 84, *loc. cit.* p. 184.
15. Cf. Paralipomena 157, *loc. cit.* p. 224.
16. "Vier Jahreszeiten," Weimarer Ausgabe I, 1, p. 352.
17. *Wilhelm Meisters Lehrjahre,* Hamburger Ausgabe 7, p. 98.
18. *Op. cit.,* p. 515.
19. Wilhelm Hertz, *Natur und Geist in Goethes Faust,* Frankfurt/M., 1931.

About the Author

Wilhelm Emrich is professor of German language and literature at the Free University of Berlin. His first important work, *Die Symbolik von Faust II*, published in 1943, established his reputation as an outstanding scholar in the field of philological research.

His most famous work, *Franz Kafka: A Critical Study of His Writings* (1958), was the outgrowth of intensive studies in modern literature at the Universities of Göttingen and Cologne. This book was issued in English in 1968.

Professor Emrich is the author of many books and essays, dealing with such literary figures as Goethe, Schiller, Eichendorff, and Kafka, as well as various aspects of literature and aesthetic criticism, including analyses of the works of many contemporary writers.